METAL CLAY
JEWELRY WORKSHOP

Handcrafted designs & techniques

METAL CLAY
JEWELRY WORKSHOP

Sian Hamilton

First published 2015 by
Guild of Master Craftsman Publications Ltd
Castle Place, 166 High Street, Lewes,
East Sussex BN7 1XU

Step photography by the jewelry designers; all other
photography by Laurel Guilfoyle.

Each contributor has been acknowledged alongside
their project.

ISBN 978 1 78494 046 1

While every effort has been made to obtain permission
from the copyright holders for all material used in
this book, the publishers will be pleased to hear from
anyone who has not been appropriately acknowledged
and to make the correction in future reprints.

The publishers and author can accept no legal
responsibility for any consequences arising from the
application of information, advice or instructions given
in this publication.

A catalog record for this book is available from the
British Library.

Publisher Jonathan Bailey
Production Manager Jim Bulley
Senior Project Editor Dominique Page
Editor Judith Chamberlain-Webber
Managing Art Editor Gilda Pacitti
Art Editor Luana Gobbo

Set in ITC Century BT
Color origination by GMC Reprographics
Printed and bound by in China

Contents

INTRODUCTION

Metal clay is a fairly new material, and has opened up the world of metal jewelry to beginners. Up until the mid 1990s, if you wanted to make jewelry with metals then you had to learn traditional metalsmithing skills, such as piercing and soldering. But with the development of metal clays it is now possible to create amazing metal jewelry with a few basic tools. Silver clay after firing is 99.9 percent pure, so it can even be hallmarked.

I am Sian Hamilton and I have been making jewelry for over 30 years. From the plastic string of beads I made as a child and wore with pride through to a BA (honours) degree in 3D design specializing in jewelry, I have been immersed in design my entire life. These days I make and sell jewelry by commission, write books about jewelry making, and am also the editor of a magazine for jewelry makers called *Making Jewellery*. The magazine has many amazingly talented designers creating beautiful projects. It is these designers that have created the stunning projects in this book.

Metal clay is one of my favorite materials to work with. As a traditionally trained jeweler I've spent many hours cutting and texturing silver to make into jewelry. So when I came across silver clay in the late 90s I loved it immediately and have been using it ever since. Fast-forward 20 years and now there are many companies making clay with a wide variety of metals (bronze, copper, steel, and more). This fabulous material presents limitless possibilities for you to explore, so familiarize yourself with the techniques, have a go at the projects in this book, then allow your imagination to run free and experiment with your own designs. I hope you enjoy it as much as I do.

Tools & Equipment

The following pages show you the most commonly used tools and equipment needed to make the projects in this book.

ESSENTIAL TOOLS

1 Roller and spacers

Any long, straight rod can be used as a rolling pin. Spacers are plastic bars with a set depth, so you can achieve an evenly rolled sheet of clay by placing them either side of the clay before rolling. Playing cards can also be used either side of the clay in place of spacers.

2 Work surface

You will need a flat, nonstick work surface for these projects. Teflon sheet is widely available and is a good flexible, nonstick surface that you can place on your worktable.

3 Tissue blade

These blades are razor sharp on one long edge. They often don't have marks to show which edge is sharp so it's a good idea to mark the sharp edge yourself with a permanent marker pen. They come in various lengths and also with a ripple (wavy) effect.

4 Shape cutters

Made from metal or plastic, these cutters come in a wide variety of shapes and can be found in places selling sugarcraft supplies as well as craft stores. Some look like cookie cutters and others have plungers. Look out for tiny straws to use for making holes in wet clay—coffee shops often have them as stirrers.

5 Texture makers

Texture plates have patterns inlayed into them that transfer onto the clay. You can use anything to make a texture on clay, such as sponges, fabric, or lace. It is essential that you coat the mats with a release agent, such as olive oil or Badger balm.

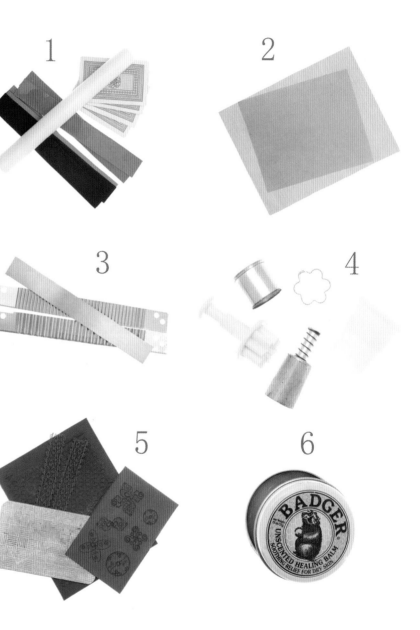

6 Release agents

Metal clay will stick to everything so you need something to help it release. Badger balm is a solid balm for dry skin so great for you as well as on metal clay. Olive oil is a cheap alternative that is already in most kitchens. There are many branded alternatives and some come as pump sprays that can be good for deep textures to make sure the release agent gets into every corner. Coat the roller, texture plates, fingers, and your work surface with a tiny amount before you start working.

USEFUL TOOLS

1 Needle tool
Used for poking holes in clay and cutting around shapes, this tool has a sharp, pointed end so use carefully.

2 Craft knife
It's useful to have something such as a scalpel blade to cut around shapes.

3 Pin vise and drill bits
This is a handheld tool for drilling holes with drill bits into metal clay.

4 Extruder
This tool comes with discs with different shapes cut out. The clay goes in the tube and you twist the handle to extrude the clay through the disc, which forms a long snake in the shape of the disc.

5 Templates
Shape templates are useful and come in a vast range of shapes. Often these are clear plastic sheets with one shape in varying sizes. Use them with a needle tool to cut the shape out of a sheet of clay.

6 Rubber block
Solid rubber blocks come as a long rectangle or square. They are good to rest dry clay pieces on when drilling or sanding as the rubber supports the clay.

7 Needle files
These are very fine, small, steel files that are used with traditional metalsmithing techniques and can be very useful with metal clay.

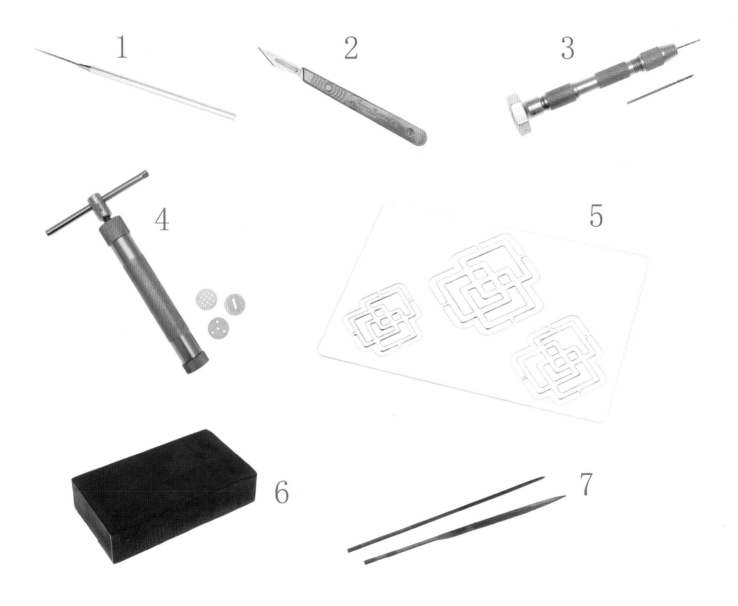

FIRING AND POLISHING

1 Kiln
Metal clay kilns are small tabletop ovens. They can go up to around 2000°F (1093°C) and are used to fire metal clay, small glass pieces, and lampwork beads. Many come with a built-in programmer, which is a really good thing to have as you can just set the program and leave the kiln to do its job. Most small kilns also run off standard household plugs and voltage.

2 Fiber blanket
This is a sheet of flexible glass fiber that you use in a kiln to support the metal clay pieces while they fire. All metal clay that is not being fired in carbon should be supported by something or it could collapse while firing.

3 Vermiculite
Vermiculite is used as a support when firing uneven shapes in the kiln. It can be placed in a pot or straight onto the kiln shelf. It will not burn.

4 Firing pans and carbon-coconut shell
When firing many base metal clays, such as copper or bronze, you need to place them in carbon that is made from coconut shells (activated carbon). The carbon needs something to sit in with a lid, so steel firing pans are used. Ceramic firing pans are also available.

5 Handheld gas torch
Small torches that can be used to fire silver and gold clays (and some brands of base metal clays) are widely available and often used in the kitchen. They work with lighter fuel that is also used in cigarette lighters.

6 Heatproof board
If using a torch, you will also need a heatproof board. These are fireproof so you can direct the flame straight onto them and they will not burn. Sometimes they are solid brick ventilated with tiny holes. If using one of these, you will need something under it that is also heatproof.

7 Insulated tweezers
If you torch fire your clay, you'll need insulated tweezers to move the clay piece after firing.

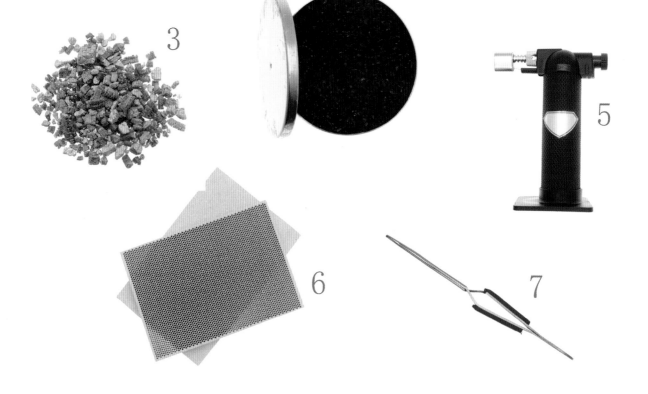

8 Tumble polisher

This is a machine that has a barrel in which you put steel shot and the fired metal pieces with water. It's then set on rollers that turn at a slow continuous speed to force the shot to roll around rubbing against the metal to make it shiny. The basic version is like the one pictured. They can vary in size and price, but if you make a lot of pieces it's worth investing in one as they save a lot of time if you like to have polished pieces.

9 Polishing papers

These papers have a micron-graded abrasive bonded to the surface. They can be folded up and used like traditional sandpaper or wrapped around paint sticks or dowels to create the shape you need. If you use them all in sequence you can achieve a very high shine, though it does take patience.

10 Burnisher

Pictured is an agate polisher, but they also come as a metal version. They are used to rub metal edges smooth.

11 Brass or steel brush

If you like a satin finish, a brass brush will create this on metal pieces straight after firing. Steel brushes are also available although they are much stiffer and will leave more marks on the metal.

12 Rotary tool

This is a small, handheld electric tool that comes with different accessories to sand, drill, and polish small metal clay pieces.

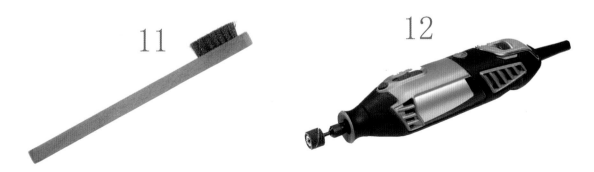

ADDITIONAL EQUIPMENT

1 Emery paper

Metal clay sands very easily before it's fired and foam-backed emery paper (sometimes known as polishing pads) is good for metal clay as it can be cut into small pieces. It can also be washed and reused. Standard wet and dry paper is also good for sanding things that need to be perfectly flat. Emery board nail files work well too as a basic sanding tool.

2 Mandrel and stand

Used for making jewelry into a particular shape, mandrels can be made of wood, metal, or plastic. They come in a variety of shapes and sizes. Wooden mandrels can also come with a stand that is very useful when working on the mandrel to hold it in place.

3 Shaping tools

When making jewelry with metal clay, these rubber-tipped shaping tools can be very useful. They come in a variety of sizes and hardness types. The soft ones work well for repairing cracks in dried pieces using paste and the harder ones are good for shaping wet clay.

4 Small paintbrush

A small, fine-pointed paintbrush is a good tool to use with paste.

5 Carving tools

These tools come in a variety of shapes and sizes. Try to find the smallest ones for use when carving dried clay. They are often called dockyard tools.

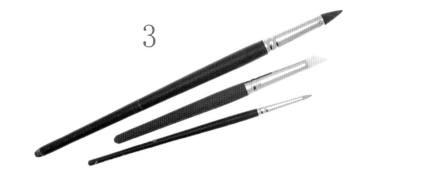

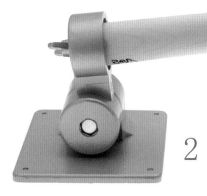

6 Molds & molding compound

Rubber molds are available to buy in a wide variety of shapes. You can also make your own by using two-part molding compound and pressing your chosen item into the rubber.

7 Polystyrene sheet

Polystyrene can be purchased in thin, lightweight sheets from hobby stores. It is easy to draw on with a ballpoint pen or round-end tool. The pattern will then transfer onto clay in the same way as any other texture sheet.

8 Adhesive

Two-part epoxy resins work well with metal clay. Cyanoacrylate glue (superglue) doesn't stick very well.

JEWELRY ASSEMBLY TOOLS

1 Pliers

There are many types of pliers available that do different jobs. The ones that are used most when starting out are round-nose (pictured), flat-nose, and chain-nose pliers.

2 Side cutters

A pair of side cutters is essential when putting jewelry pieces together, because they are used to cut off any excess wire.

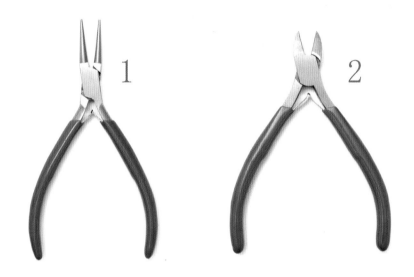

Materials

The projects in this book are made using materials that are widely available.

METAL CLAY

Metal clay comes in a variety of forms; all are the same basic material but used to do different things.

1 Lump clay

The solid form of metal clay that looks like putty is called lump clay. It is made up of very fine particles of metal mixed with an organic binder that burns off in firing leaving a solid metal piece. It can be rolled, molded, textured, and colored. This type of clay is available in many metals—the most common are fine silver (999), Sterling silver (925), copper, and bronze.

2 Paper clay

Paper clay is only available in fine silver from the two main brands, Precious Metal Clay and Art Clay. This is the only type that cannot be torch-fired. It's also unique as it does not dry out but remains a flexible sheet. It can be used with any other type of clay.

3 Syringe clay

This type of clay is a paste already in a tube that you can use to embellish pieces or as a glue to stick sections of a project together.

4 Paste

Paste is a softer, more liquid version of lump clay. It can be watered down to make it a "slip". Different brands of paste do different things, so it's best to work with the same brand of paste that goes with the brand of metal clay you choose. You can also make your own paste by watering down lump clay.

5 Powdered clay

You need to add water to powdered clays; they then work in exactly the same way as lump clay. This type of clay is available in many metals, including steel, silver, bronze, and copper.

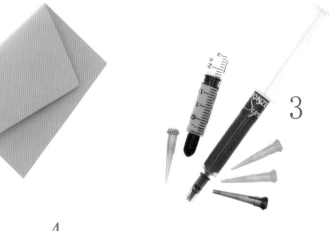

COLORING FIRED CLAY

1 Gilders paste

This is a highly concentrated, wax-based medium available in a wide range of colors. It is resistant to water and can be used on many materials. This paste has a strong smell and should be used in a well-ventilated area.

2 Resin and mica powder

Clear resin works well with fine powders such as mica. Resin dries in the air and has the appearance of glass. Mix it with metallic powders such as mica to color the surface of metal clay after it is fired. Use resin only in well-ventilated areas.

3 Enamel paints

Enamel paints should not be confused with ground-glass enamel that needs to be heated. Enamel paints are solvent-based paints in bright colors and come in a range of effects such as pearl and metallic. They are painted onto the fired surface of the piece and take around three days to completely dry. They should be used in a well-ventilated area.

4 Liver of sulfur

This is a chemical that darkens metal like silver and copper. It doesn't work on metals like gold or brass. It works by being mixed with water, and then the jewelry piece to be darkened is dipped in the solution and left for as long as you want. The jewelry will get darker the longer it stays in the solution. To stop the reaction, the jewelry needs to be washed in soapy water. It can be removed by polishing it off with a silver or metal polishing cloth.

THE REST

1 Polymer clay

It is useful to have a little polymer around to help work out structures before getting metal clay out of the packet. It can also help when drying shapes to rest the clay over.

2 Glass cabochons and embeddable stones

Round glass domes (called cabochons) and faceted crystals can be purchased to embed in the clay and fire in place. Look out for the ones that say fireable. Not all crystals can take the heat. If you are using fireable stones, then never cool fired clay pieces by dunking in water, because the stones will shatter. Leave them to cool naturally.

3 Embeddable findings

These are metal findings that have been specially made to be embedded in raw clay and fired in place. They have a stalk that goes into the clay and the loop sits on the outside.

FINDINGS

Findings are the items that you need to make your metal clay pieces into jewelry. These include:

1 Clasps

There are many different types of clasp available, including slides, bolts, triggers, and even magnetic varieties. Choose a clasp to suit your design.

2 Jumprings

A jumpring is a single ring of wire that is used to join pieces together. They come in every size you can think of and many different colors.

3 Headpins and eyepins

These are pieces of wire with a flat or ball end (headpin) or a loop at the end (eyepin). Thread a bead on the wire and make a loop at the open end to secure the bead in place. Eyepins can be linked together to make a chain.

4 Earwires

Earwires come in various styles, from a simple "U" shape with a loop, to ones with a bead and coil finish. The loop is opened to thread on the earring piece.

5 Crimp beads and covers

Crimp beads look like small metal beads with large holes or tubes. They work by compressing stringing materials together to hold them in place. Used with crimp beads, crimp covers go over the crimp to make it look like a normal small bead. They come in a variety of metal color finishes.

1

3

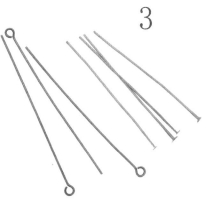

5

2

4

STRINGING MATERIALS, WIRE, AND CHAIN

There are many things that can be used to string your metal clay pieces into necklaces or bracelets including: nylon-coated beading wire, beading thread, clear elastic, tiger tail, leather, cotton thong, and suede.

1 Nylon-coated beading wire

This wire is available in a range of brands and is really good for stringing, as it has a better strength for heavy pieces than ordinary threads. It also holds a nice shape on the neck.

2 Leather/cord/suede

These types of cords come in various colors and thicknesses. They can be knotted securely with ease or used with ribbon crimps or neck ends.

3 Wire

Wire comes in a large range of sizes. It is often referred to in the USA by gauge, and UK by millimeters, and is also sometimes known by Standard Wire Gauge (SWG). When starting out, buy plated wire, as it is much cheaper than precious metal. Look for a non-tarnishing variety so it doesn't discolor against your skin.

4 Chain

There are many styles of chain and a variety of colors available. Fine chains are good for hanging pendants and large-link chains are good for making charm bracelets or when adding beads to the individual links.

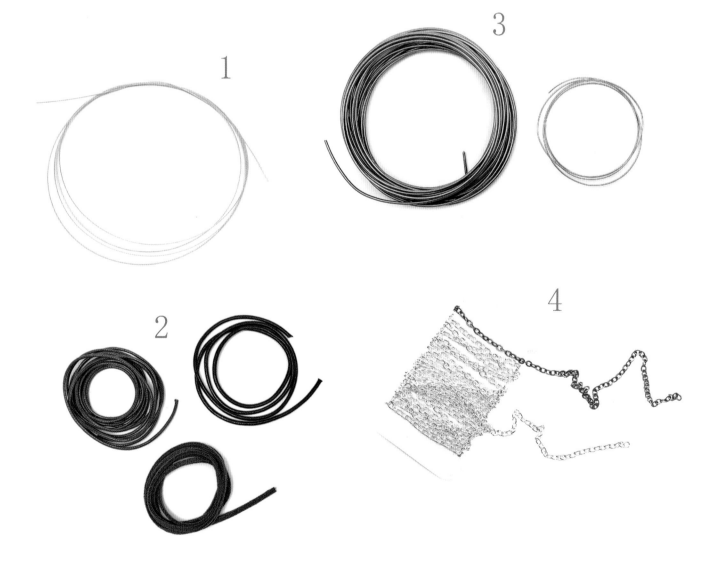

Metal Clay Techniques

Here are some of the basic techniques needed to work successfully with metal clay and complete the projects in this book.

Rolling, texturing, and cutting shapes

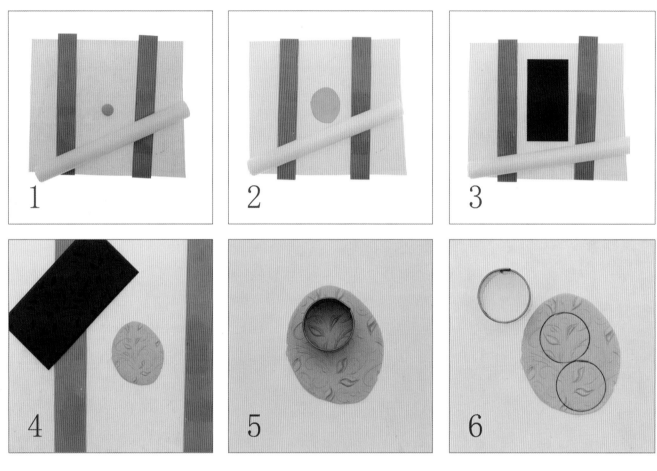

The most basic technique to master when using metal clay is rolling it out to an even thickness. Metal clays will dry out quickly so work with small pieces and keep the rest sealed tightly in the packet.

1 Take a small piece of clay and place on your nonstick surface. Place the right-size spacers (or stacks of playing cards) for the thickness you want either side of the clay.

2 Take a roller and rub a small amount of oil or Badger balm over it while also coating your fingers. Roll firmly until the clay is the same thickness as the spacers. If texturing, do not remove the sheet from the nonstick surface.

3 Rub a little oil or balm over the texture plate, making sure there is oil in every crevice, and place over the clay with the texture side down. Roll firmly from the end closest to you up to the far end. Do not roll back over.

4 If you have used enough oil or balm then when you pick up the plate the clay should stay on the nonstick surface. Gently peel the clay off the nonstick surface. If you are going to cut shapes in the sheet then lay the texture back down on the nonstick surface with the texture facing up.

5 To cut shapes, take the cutter you want to use and rub a tiny amount of oil or balm over the cutting edge. Place the cutter down on the clay then press firmly straight down.

6 When you can feel that the cutter has gone through the clay, give it a very slight wiggle to help the shape release from the sheet. Pull the cutter out.

Cutting holes with a straw

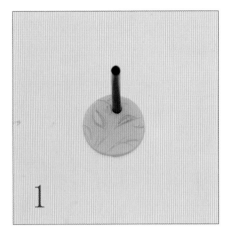

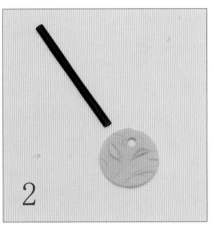

You can make holes in wet clay pieces using a straw or small round cutter.

1 If you are cutting holes when it is wet then do it straight after cutting the shapes out, before you move the shapes off the nonstick surface. Take a small straw and cut it down to about 1in (25mm). Mark

in the clay with a cocktail stick where you want the hole to be.

2 Line up the straw with the mark and press straight down through the clay. Make sure the straw is straight. Pull the straw out—if there is clay stuck in the straw, then poke it out with the cocktail stick and wrap up the scrap.

Drilling a hole in dry clay

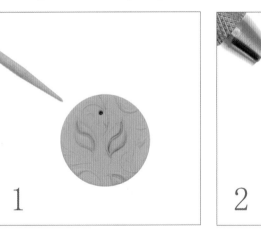

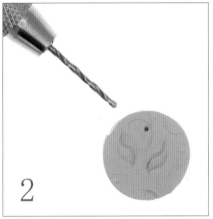

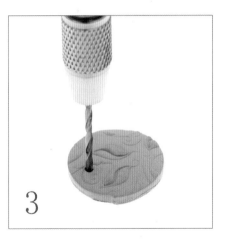

You can also make holes by waiting until the pieces of clay are completely dry and drill them with a pin vise and drill bit. Drilling gives a more precise finish but does take a little more skill.

1 While the clay is still wet, mark where you want the hole to be with a cocktail stick. Allow the clay to dry completely.

2 Place the drill bit into the pin vise. Use a drill bit that's about 15–20 percent bigger than you want the hole to be

as the hole will shrink with the clay when it's fired. If drilling something flat then use a rubber block to support the clay. If the shape you are drilling is three-dimensional then hold it in your fingers. Remember that the moisture in your skin will transfer into the clay making it soft again, so hold it gently and dry the piece afterward.

3 Pin vises work by placing the end of the vise in your palm and rolling the shank of the vise between your first finger and thumb. Position the drill bit on the mark in the clay. Turn the pin vise very slowly—the weight of your hand and the pin vise will be enough to cut through the clay, so don't push. Work slowly and you will be able to feel when the drill has gone all the way through. Keep checking that the bit is going in the direction you want and adjust as you go.

Firing clay with a handheld gas torch

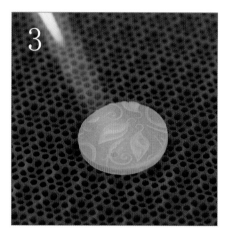

Using a handheld gas torch is a quick and cheap method of firing metal clay. It only takes about three minutes to make a clay piece into metal. The final metal piece will not be as strong as a kiln-fired piece and may possibly break if put under stress.

1   Take a heatproof block and place the metal piece to be fired on it. Get a glass or ceramic bowl and fill with cold water and place within reach to one side. Also have a pair of insulated tweezers to hand. Get a timer and set for three minutes and 30 seconds.

2   Light the torch and reduce the light in the room if you can, because this will help you see the color the clay needs to achieve. Turn on the timer. Wave the torch across the metal clay to light the binder. It will catch light easily and create a flame. This is normal so let it burn off—the flame will go out very quickly.

3   You now need to concentrate the flame on the piece, moving the flame in a circular motion so it's not on one area for too long. The piece needs to achieve a red glow (the color of raw salmon) but not to go so far that the piece starts to get a bright neon glow (at that point you risk melting the whole piece). It needs to glow for 3 minutes (minimum) to become a solid metal. When the timer goes off, pick the piece up with the insulated tweezers and drop into the cold water.

Making a texture plate

Thin polystyrene is great for making your own texture plates and is widely available from craft stores.

1   Take a sheet of polystyrene and a pen. The width of the line you create will relate to the size of the end of the pen. So if you want fine lines then you will need a fine-pointed pen. You can also use a ball-ended burnisher or pencil.

2   Draw the pattern you want onto the sheet. Draw lightly to start with to lay the pattern out. Remember that the lines you draw will become the raised part of the clay design.

3   When you are happy with the pattern, go over the lines and push a little harder to deepen the lines. You can vary the depth to get a variation of height on the pattern. You can make lines thicker too to suit your design.

4   When you have finished the design, cut it out with scissors leaving a good size border. The rest of the polystyrene sheet is ready for another texture and you have a finished texture plate that is easy to handle. Polystyrene sheet is nonstick so you don't need to add a release agent to it, just use it as it is.

Firing clay with a kiln

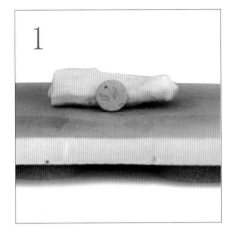

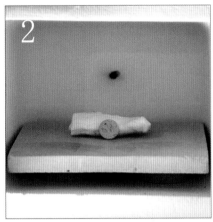

If you are going to make a lot of jewelry with metal clay then it's wise to invest in a kiln. Kiln firing will make your metal pieces as strong as they can get and will give consistent results. Always follow the firing instructions provided with the kiln.

1 The kiln should be placed in a well-ventilated area and on a heatproof surface. Start by placing your pieces to be fired on a kiln shelf. If the pieces are flat then they can just be placed directly on the shelf. If they have a three-dimensional form, then any pieces that are raised will need to be supported by a fiber blanket or vermiculite.

2 Place the kiln shelf in the kiln. Close the door and set the programmer following the manufacturer's instructions. Refer to the clay manufacturer's information to see what temperature is required and how long the clay needs to be fired. Most instructions will give a temperature the kiln needs to reach and then a soak time (how long the kiln needs to hold the temperature).

3 When the kiln has completed the soak, the programmer will turn off and the kiln will start to cool. You can speed up the cooling process by opening the door a crack. Don't touch the inside or any of the metal pieces with your bare hands, as it will all be very hot. If you want to remove pieces while the kiln is still hot, use heatproof gloves and be really careful. If you drop anything on the floor it could melt your floor covering. Have a bowl of cold water by the kiln and drop the metal straight into the water to cool (this is called quenching). If you have time, it is safest to let the kiln go cold with the metal inside.

Making a mold

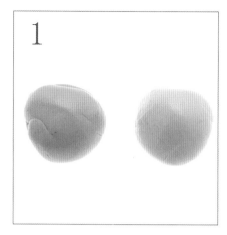

It's nice to make your own molds, and very easy with two-part modeling compound. Once these compounds are mixed they start going hard immediately so you must work fast.

1 Decide what you want to make a mold of and place it close to hand. Measure out equal amounts of each part of the modeling compound. Make sure you are pretty precise, as the rubber won't go off properly if you don't have equal amounts. Mix the two together until it's one uniform color and you cannot see any stripes. Roll it into a ball then flatten it slightly.

2 Push the item you want to make a mold of into the flattened ball and push the rubber up against the sides of the item. Try to be precise here and look at how the item is sitting to check if you have undercuts that could cause a problem.

3 Leave to go off for about 5 minutes. To check that the rubber has gone off, press your fingernail into the rubber. If it has gone off and hardened, the fingernail will not make an indent. Pull the molded piece out of the rubber and the mold is ready to use.

Making clay pieces

1 Take a piece of fresh lump clay out of the packet and push firmly into the mold so that it fills all the space. Try to get it level with the top of the mold and be as neat as possible; it will save you lots of time later.

2 Let the clay dry completely, and then gently press the back of the mold to push the clay out.

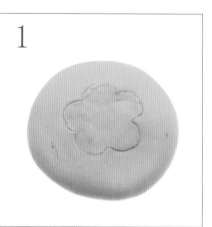

Using liver of sulfur

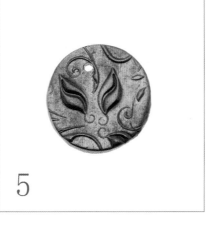

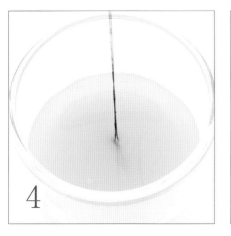

Liver of sulfur (LOS) is a substance used as a patina for darkening metals. It works on silver, copper, and bronze.

1 To use LOS you will need two water containers (for the step photos I've used small glasses but you can use anything that can take water, and that you don't use with food), a pair of plastic tweezers, and some paper tissue. It is important that you follow the safety instructions that come with LOS, so you will also need safety glasses and gloves. Always work in a well-ventilated area, because although LOS is nontoxic, it does smell very bad!

2 Clean the item to be colored in hot soapy water to wash off any grease or residue from the making process. Thread a piece of cotton through a hole in the piece.

3 Fill both of the water containers, one with cold water and one with warm water from the faucet. Do not use boiling water. You can use LOS with cold water; it just takes a lot longer for the color to develop. Fill both containers about halfway. You only need a few drops of LOS for this process; the stronger the solution the blacker the results.

4 Dip the piece on the thread into the LOS—make sure the whole piece is covered or the patina will not develop evenly. Hold it in the solution until it turns the color you want it to go. If you are not sure, periodically take it out and dunk it in the cold water to stop the coloring process and take a look at the piece. You can keep going back to the LOS solution as many times as you like.

5 When the piece is the color you require, dip it into another container with water mixed with a little baking soda to neutralize the LOS. Then wash thoroughly under the faucet with liquid dish soap and warm water.

6 Let the piece air dry and then polish with a polishing cloth to take the patina off the top surface. LOS is great for defining patterns, and polishing off the dark color from the surface of the piece helps to make the patterns clearer. Over time, this patina can go darker or lighter, so to avoid this, coat with a layer of wax.

Jewelry Techniques

Opening and closing a jumpring

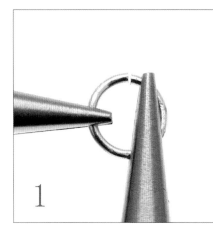

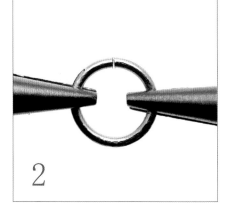

To make sure that jumprings shut securely, it is important to know how to open and close them correctly. You will need two pairs of pliers with flat jaws, chain-nose, flat-nose or nylon-nose will work.

1 Take a jumpring in two pairs of pliers with the opening centered at the top. Holding the jumpring this way—with one pair of pliers across one side of the ring—helps to stabilize large rings.

2 You can also hold the pliers this way with both pairs facing inward. Both ways are fine, and the way you need to attach the jumpring often dictates which way you hold it.

3 Hold the jumping on both sides and twist one hand toward you and the other hand away. This will keep the ring round in shape. Reverse the action to close the ring. Don't ever pull the ring apart as that will warp the shape. Use this technique to open loops on eyepins too.

If you find that pliers mark the jumprings, wrap a bit of masking tape around the ends.

Making a simple loop

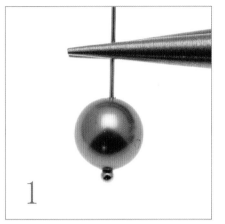

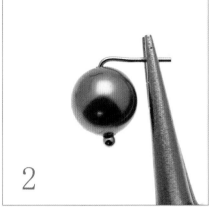

Loops have a multitude of functions in making jewelry, so forming them properly is a skill worth mastering. A simple (sometimes called open) loop can be opened and closed to allow them to be attached and detached as desired.

1 Thread a bead onto a headpin or eyepin and cut the pin about ⅜in (10mm) above the bead.

2 Bend the wire to a right angle above the bead.

3 Using round-nose pliers, grasp the wire at the very end and curl it around the plier jaws.

4 Roll the wire around to meet the bead.

5 Move the plier jaws around the loop to sit by the bead, away from the open end. Bend the loop back to sit directly above the bead.

6 Use chain-nose pliers to tighten the loop by wiggling it until the gap is closed.

Making a wrapped loop

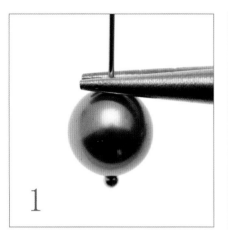

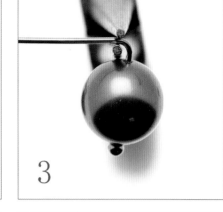

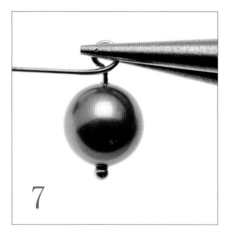

This style of loop is the most secure—once attached it cannot be removed unless it is cut off.

1   Thread a bead onto a headpin or eyepin. Grip the wire with round-nose pliers next to the bead.

2   Bend the wire above the plier jaw to a right angle. You will need about ¹⁄₁₆in (2mm) of wire above the bead before the bend.

3   Move the plier jaws to sit at the top of the bend.

4   Use your thumb to push the wire back around the pliers, keeping it tight to the jaw.

5   Keep pushing the wire around the jaw until you meet the bead.

6   Move the pliers around the loop to hold it close to the open side and continue to bend the wire around until it is facing out at a right angle and you have a complete loop.

7   If adding the loop to chain or a jumpring, thread the loop onto the chain at this stage. Use a pair of chain-nose pliers to hold across the loop firmly. Make sure any chain or ring is above the pliers.

8

9

10

8 Wrap the wire around the neck of the loop until it meets the bead.

9 Use side cutters to snip off any excess wire. Make sure the flat side of the cutter jaws is facing the coil.

10 Take the chain-nose pliers and push the cut end of the wire into the coil, so that it sits flush.

Attaching loops

1

2

Attaching a clasp to the end of a necklace or attaching beaded pieces made on eyepins is simple and makes an attractive chain.

1 Take two pairs of chain-nose, or other flat-jaw pliers and open the loop on a beaded piece by holding the side away from the opening steady and twisting the open side toward or away from you (the same way as in the opening jumprings technique on page 26). Only open the loop as far as you need to thread on other loops.

2 Attach the next loop or a jumpring and close the loop by reversing the twist. Don't pull the loop outward or it will distort.

Aztec Armor

This striking and stylish copper design for a necklace and matching earrings, by Nicola Beer, was inspired by the metalwork of Aztec artisans.

FOR THE NECKLACE YOU WILL NEED

50g Art Clay Copper

10 x 10mm copper jumprings (made from US 18-gauge SWG 19, 1mm wire)

18in (46cm) length of thick copper chain with clasp

Parchment paper

Pencil

Badger balm

Teflon or other nonstick work surface

Acrylic roller

Playing cards or spacer bars

Texture mat

Needle tool or craft knife

1.25mm drill bit and pin vise

Sanding pads or emery paper

Safety pickle

Rubber block

Brass brush

Steel block

Rawhide or nylon hammer

Ball pein hammer

Gilders paste in Patina

Stiff paintbrush or sponge

White spirit

Soft lint-free polishing cloth

Pliers

Liver of sulfur (optional)

Necklace

1. Begin by deciding the size of your necklace, then draw a bib or crescent moon-shaped template, in five sections, onto a piece of greaseproof paper. As we are using copper clay you will also need to account for shrinkage of the final fired pieces. Check the fired shrinkage rate on your brand to ensure that your template is the correct size.

2. Cut out the sections of your paper template. Lightly balm a nonstick surface and evenly roll out a ball of copper clay to a thickness of five playing cards or 1/16in (1.5mm) (see page 20). Apply balm to the back of your template; this will help you to gently stick it to the clay and will ensure it doesn't slip. Use either a needle tool or a sharp craft knife to cut around the template. Remove the paper and set this piece aside to dry. Repeat this process for four sections, leaving the central section until last.

3. To texture the central section, roll a piece of clay to six cards or 1/8in (2mm) thick onto a well-balmed surface. Lubricate a texture mat with plenty of balm and lay the rolled out clay on top of it. Gently roll across the clay until you have an even, well defined imprint. Release the clay and place it on your surface, texture side up. Cut out the last piece of template.

4. Let the five sections air dry for 24 hours. It is important that there is no moisture remaining in the clay when it is fired. To test if it is dried, place the clay onto a mirror and look for condensation. If there is moisture present, further drying time is needed. Test that your pieces fit nicely together and, using a pencil, mark on the back of your work where you are going to drill holes to attach the pieces together.

5. Using a 1.25mm drill bit in a pin vise, gently drill out each hole as shown (see page 21). Do not be tempted to press heavily on the clay, as it is fragile at this stage and can break. Don't drill holes too close to the edges as this can also cause cracking. Sand the pieces until you are happy with the finish.

6. Fire each piece according to the instructions on your clay. There will be some hammering involved to finish the project, so it is important to ensure that the clay has turned to metal during firing (a process called sintering). If a black coating (firescale) is present after quenching, drop the copper into warmed pickle to remove. Once clean, rinse off the pickle, place the pieces onto a rubber block, and brush them vigorously with a brass brush.

7. Use a rawhide or nylon hammer to flatten out any warping of the copper that may have occurred during firing. Use a ball pein, or other hammer of your choice, on a steel block to create texture on the smooth pieces of copper. For the central section, ensure that it is perfectly flat but don't hammer it with a metal hammer, as you don't want to destroy the intricate pattern.

8. Using a stiff paintbrush, your fingers, or a sponge, apply a thick coating of gilders paste all over the patterned central section. Push it into the crevices and before it dries, wipe over the raised surface with a soft cloth, lightly moistened with white spirit. The cloth will remove the paste from the surface, leaving the recesses colored. Leave to dry for several hours, and then buff the copper with a soft cloth.

9. Attach the five sections together with the jumprings to form the necklace (see page 26). Attach chunky copper chain to the bib section. If you want to, you can also oxidize the copper with liver of sulfur to give a more antiqued look (see page 25).

Safety pickle comes as granules that you mix with water to remove oxides from metals after firing. It's a safe alternative to traditional acid.

Earrings

YOU WILL NEED

15g Art Clay copper

Art Clay copper paste

2 x earring findings

To create a pair of statement earrings, cut out two trapezoid shapes in copper clay. Use a cutter and cut out two flowers. When they are dry, use copper clay paste to adhere the flowers to the trapezoid shapes. Drill a hole in the top of each earring for a finding and fire according to the manufacturer's instructions. Add earwires (see Attaching a loop on page 29).

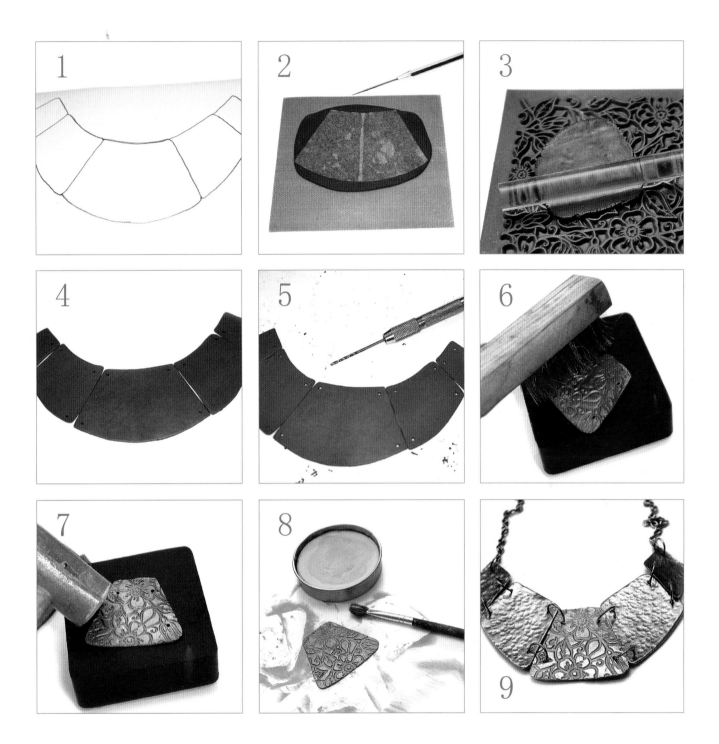

Gilders paste is excellent for adding color to all metals and comes in a wide range of hues. Experiment by combining several colors for dramatic effects.

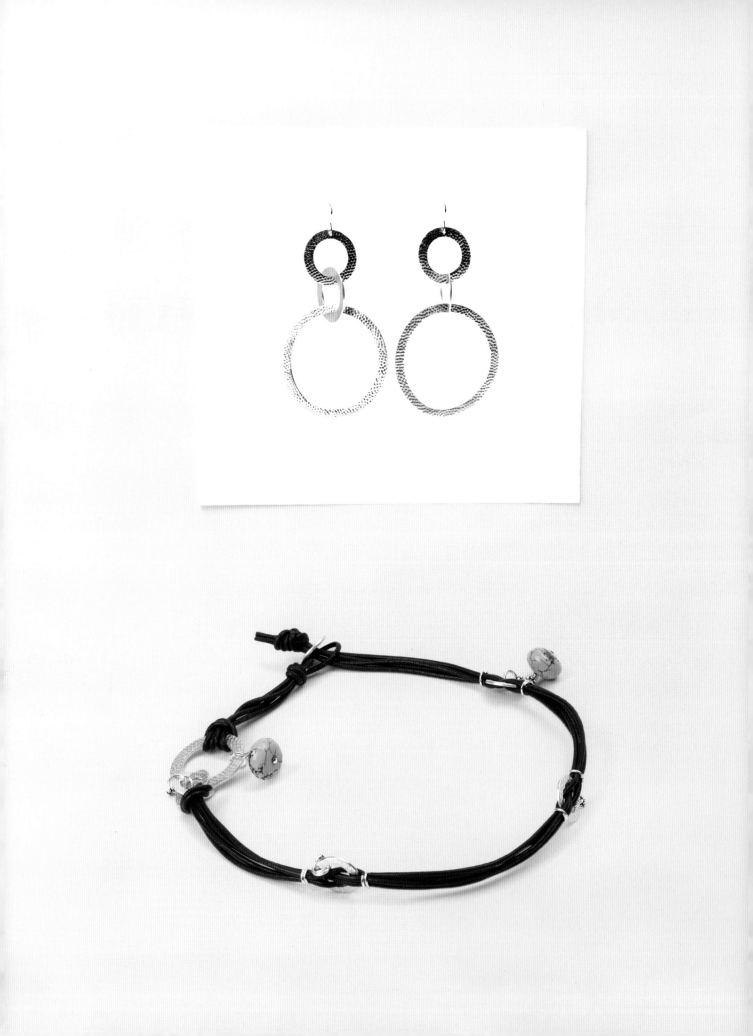

Loop the Hoop

Candy Chappill shows you a simple but effective technique to make metal clay linked hoops. Use it to make these statement earrings and adapt it to make the leather bracelet.

FOR THE EARRINGS YOU WILL NEED

15g Art Clay silver

Art Clay silver syringe

2 x earwires

Roller

1mm spacer bars

Texture sheet (optional)

Round cookie cutters

Badger balm or olive oil

Craft knife

Rubber block

Swivel pin vise

1.5mm drill bit and pin vise

180-grit sanding sponge

Firing method

Vermiculite

Brass brush

Chain- and flat-nose pliers

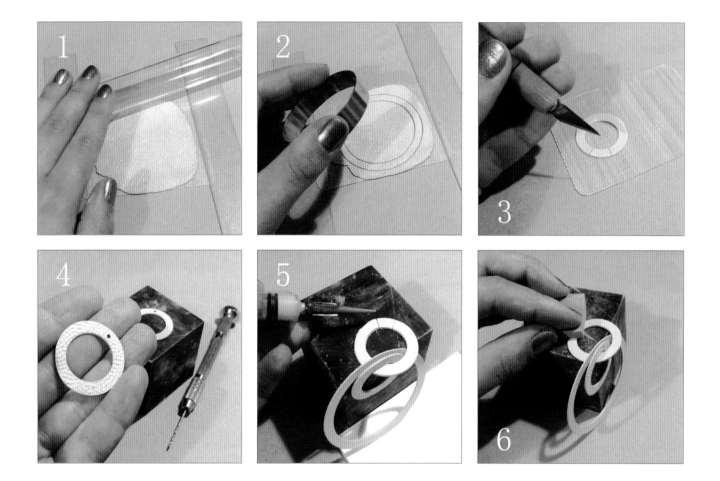

Earrings

1 Roll out your clay ¹⁄₃₂in (1mm) thick (see page 20). Use a texture sheet for a subtle hammered texture look. If you decide to use a texture sheet, make sure you place your spacers on top of the sheet and not next to it. This will avoid your clay becoming too thin.

2 Cut out two smaller hoops and one larger hoop using various sized cookie cutters. Remember to add some Badger balm or olive oil to your cutters to stop them sticking to the clay.

3 With one of your smaller hoops, cut out a small section using your craft knife. The smaller and neater you can get this cut now, the easier it will be for you later. Once you have cut it out, don't try and move it, just let it dry.

4 Once your pieces are dry, drill a ¹⁄₁₆in (1.5mm) hole in two of your smaller hoops (see page 21). This is for attaching the earwires later on. It's best to use a rubber block to lean on when you drill—this helps to support your piece.

5 Remove the already cut section from your smaller hoop and carefully thread your other hoops onto it. Place the removed section back in place and syringe around the join. Again, this is a lot easier to do if you support your pieces on a rubber block.

6 Once your syringe is dry, sand down any rough edges using the sanding sponge. You may need to add some more syringe and then repeat this stage until you cannot see the join any more. You want a seamless finish.

7 Once you are happy with your join, fire your pieces in a kiln at 1,472°F (800°C) for half an hour (see page 23). Using vermiculite as a bed for the earrings helps to support them during firing. Lay them on the shelf with some slack between the hoops.

8 After firing, use a brass brush to bring up to a satin shine. You can use any other polishing method you want though. Try tumbling your pieces for a gorgeous high shine.

9 Finally hang your hoops onto their earwires using both pairs of pliers to open and close the loops (see page 29). If you want studs then you can skip Step 4 and solder your posts onto the back of the top hoop.

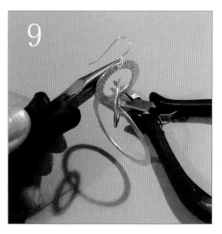

Bracelet

YOU WILL NEED

10g Art Clay silver

12 x 6mm silver jumprings

6 x 4mm daisy spacer beads

2 x 1in (25mm) silver headpins

2 x 8mm turquoise beads

48in (1.2m) length of 1mm brown leather cord

Cut three pieces of leather cord 16in (41cm) long and set to one side. Now make six small silver hoops and one large one using the main steps. Two small hoops and the large one should be connected as if you were making an earring. The other four small hoops should be single and one hoop should have a ¼in (6mm) hole in the middle (no larger). Fire and finish them completely.

Take two of the pieces of leather and fold them in half, then pass the two folds through the end small silver hoop on the piece with three hoops attached together. Thread the cord ends through the loops in the leather and pull tight. Thread a 6mm jumpring over all four pieces of cord then add a silver hoop. Thread two cords through the silver hoop from one side and the other two from the opposite side so the cord holds the hoop securely. Move the silver hoop along the cords so it's about 3in (7.5cm) away from the end hoop.

Add another jumpring and push both jumprings until they sit either side of the hoop. Add another jumpring and another hoop, repeating the process of taking two cords through the hoop from each side.

Repeat again for a third hoop, with jumprings either side, then place the hoop with the ¼in (6mm) hole over all four cords.

You should now have a chain of three hoops at one end and three small hoops spaced along the length, with a silver hoop over all four cords. Knot these cords together about 3in (7.5cm) away from the third hoop and push the loose hoop to the end. Take the end with the large hoop attached and the spare piece of cord you cut at the beginning. Fold the cord in half and then in half again, push the end with two loops through the large hoop and feed the ends through the loop; pull tight. Finally knot the short cord so the loop can be used to pass over the end silver hoop to connect the necklace and then cut off any excess cord. Secure the knots with glue if desired.

Take the four 6mm jumprings and place a daisy spacer on each one then attach them to the silver hoops (see page 26). Add a turquoise bead to each headpin and make a simple loop at the ends (see page 27). Attach one of these to the large hoop and the other to one of the other small hoops using the last two 6mm jumprings.

You don't need to texture the middle hoop, because it can be very tricky to join it back up and keep the texture intact.

Tangerine Dreams

This gorgeous bracelet in silver clay by Tracey Spurgin has a beautiful enameled splash of color for added zing. You can make earrings and a pendant to match too.

FOR THE BRACELET YOU WILL NEED

30g Art Clay silver

Art Clay silver paste

Pebeo Fantasy Moon paint

Roller

1mm spacer bars

Badger balm or olive oil

Craftworx design template (2315)

Needle tool

0.75mm spacer bars

Paintbrush

Needle files

Emery paper

Polishing papers

Brass tube

Handheld gas torch or kiln (optional)

Tumble polisher or radial disc on a rotary tool

Liver of sulfur

Fine needle

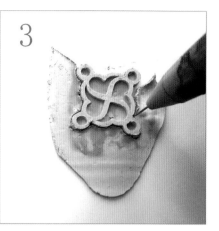

Bracelet

1 On a prepared work surface, roll out the clay to ¹⁄₃₂in (1mm) thick (see page 20). Lightly balm the template with Badger balm to prevent it from sticking to the clay. Dip the needle tool into the balm to help the tool glide through the clay, as you pierce out the design. Leave to dry.

2 Repeat the piercing to make enough designs for the bracelet. Make an extra piece, but this time pierce out the center bars; this will become the toggle clasp for fastening the bracelet. Once all the frames are dry, gently sand and file each piece to make the surface level and flat.

3 To make the backing, roll out the clay to ¹⁄₃₂in (1mm) thick. Use a paintbrush to apply a little water. Place the frame onto the wet clay. Very gently press down the frame onto the wet clay. Using the needle tool, once again pierce around the outer edge of the frame. Remove the excess clay and place to dry.

4 Sand and clean each of the component parts with files, grits, and polishing papers.

5 To create the detail of little bumps, use a brass tube or similar item you have to hand. Cut it to a manageable length and use it like a regular circle cutter. Before you cut, place plastic wrap over the top of the clay to create a clear rounded shoulder to each shape. Leave to dry.

6 Attach the bumps to the components by applying a very tiny amount of paste to the underside of the bump, put it into place, and wick away any excess paste with a water brush or a fine wet paintbrush. Leave to dry.

7 To fire the pieces, place on a gas hob or torch fire with a small handheld gas torch. Or you can fire them in a kiln at 1,472°F (800°C) for 20 minutes (see page 22).

8 The best polishing options are to use a handheld rotary tool or a tumble polisher. (You could use polishing papers, but it would take much longer to get the desired effect.) Oxidize using warm water and liver of sulfur solution (see page 25).

9 To add the color to the cells, apply Pebeo Fantasy Moon paint. To control the application of the product into the cells, pick up a tiny amount of product on a fine needle, and allow it to drip into the cell. Ensure that the pieces are level while the product dries. Allow at least 48 hours to dry and then assemble the bracelet using jumprings (see page 26).

Pendant

YOU WILL NEED

10g Art Clay silver

Pebeo Fantasy Moon paint

1 x pendant bail

1 x snake chain with clasp

Once you have rolled the clay, repeat the piercing technique to make one large piece for the wheel pendant and follow through the rest of the main steps. Attach the wheel to a bail and finally attach the bail to a snake chain.

Earrings

YOU WILL NEED

10g Art Clay silver (or scrap from main project)

Pebeo Fantasy Moon paint

2 x silver-colored earwires

In the same way, make a pair of matching earrings. Hang them from earwires by attaching one of the corners of the wheel to the loop on the earwire (see page 29).

Try making your own stencils by sketching out a design on paper. Laminate and cut out with a sharp craft knife.

Copper Coin Charm

Super simple to make, these striking African-style earrings with matching bracelet by Candy Chappill use a minimal amount of clay and are perfect for beginners and small budgets.

FOR THE EARRINGS YOU WILL NEED

10g Art Clay copper

46 x 1.8mm (size 11) turquoise seed beads

2 x large kidney copper earwires

6 x 6mm copper jumprings

Roller

Textured tile (optional)

Small round cutter

1.5mm spacer bars

Badger balm or olive oil

Tuff nonstick card

Sanding pad and baby wipe

2mm drill bit and pin vise

Fiber brick

Handheld gas torch

Tweezers

Pot of water

Brass brush

Polishing papers

Liver of sulfur

Pliers

Art Clay copper is sold only in 50g weights and since it will start to oxidize once opened, it is a good idea to try to use the whole pack as soon as possible.

Quenching the piece directly after firing is important in this project. Quenching avoids firescale altogether.

Earrings

1 Roll out the clay to ⅛in (1.5mm) thick (see page 20). You could roll it onto a textured tile, like this subtle African-style tile, to add some extra interest. Use a small cutter to cut out several small, round coins. Don't forget to add a release agent such as Badger balm or olive oil to the roller, work surface, texture tile, and cutter to stop the clay from sticking.

2 When the coins have dried, refine any rough areas using a sanding pad. Don't forget to sand the back too. You could also use a baby wipe to smooth off the edges; simply wrap around your finger and smooth over the edges and back—it works really well, and eliminates the sanding dust.

3 Using the 2mm drill bit, drill a hole in the center of all the coins (see page 21). To get a nice smooth hole, it's best to drill from the front, until you see a small dent in the back. Then turn it over and drill into the dent. This way both sides are nice and neat without any fraying.

4 To fire, place the coin on the brick and heat with a torch (see page 22). You want the coin to glow a bright orange/red. Hold this for around three minutes. While keeping the piece glowing, pick it up with tweezers in your other hand, and drop it straight into the water to quench it—this will avoid any firescale from developing. Fire the coins one at a time.

5 Once fired, brush with a brass brush, and polish it up a little bit with a polishing paper. Try brushing the piece in warm water, with a little bit of dish washing soap. For extra shine you could also use a tumble polisher.

6 Assemble your finished earrings using jumprings and earwires (see pages 26 and 29). To give the piece an antique look and to match all the different-colored copper components, use some liver of sulfur (see page 25). Simply mix a few drops with hot water, submerge your piece, and then polish off with a pro-polishing pad. Add 23 turquoise seed beads to each earwire for extra color and interest.

Bracelet

YOU WILL NEED

10g Art Clay copper

21 x 6mm copper jumprings

1 x black rubber cord necklace

Make a bunch of coins using the main steps and attach them to a rubber cord necklace for a Boho-style wraparound bracelet. Attach each one to two jumprings as in Step 6 and then attach another jumpring to the rubber cord and add on the two jumprings with the coin. Add as many as you like and add in extra jumprings on their own, for extra contrast with the black cord.

Mosaic Mode

This pair of earrings in fine silver clay by Tracey Spurgin has micro mosaic tiles embedded into resin to add a lovely, colorful detail. An eye-catching ring completes the set.

FOR THE EARRINGS YOU WILL NEED

7g Art Clay silver

2 x earwires

4 x 4mm jumprings

Sheet of baked polymer clay or polymer clay canes

10g clear resin

Roller

1.5mm spacer bars

Badger balm or olive oil

Wallpaper sample or texture sheet

1mm spacer bars

Craftworx design template 2259

Needle tool

Needle files

0.5mm spacer bars

Foam-backed emery paper and emery boards (nail files)

2mm drill bit and pin vise

Brass brush

Liver of sulfur

Polish and soft cloth

Sharp craft knife

PVA glue

Condition the clay by rolling it fast and hard in the heel of your hands. Bring the clay to a soft putty ball, with no cracks or fold lines.

Earrings

1 On a prepared work surface, roll out the clay to ¹⁄₁₆in (1.5mm) thick (see page 20). Lightly balm and texture the clay. Here a wallpaper sample placed underneath the clay creates the perfect shallow texture. Re-roll using 1mm spacers.

2 Using the Craftworx template, pierce out the smallest pattern with the needle tool. Start the piercing at the narrowest point of each of the aperture shapes. Keep the stencil in place over the clay while you pick out each piece of excess clay. This helps to support the clay and reduce any distortion in movement.

3 Next cut the outline shape of the earring. This can be done freeform or using further stencils. Repeat for the second earring. This process can be repeated to achieve large components or play around with the positioning of the stencil on the clay to create further patterns (see the ring as an example). Set the pieces to dry.

4 Once fully dried, the earring pieces need to be sanded and cleaned with needle files. The clay is very delicate at this stage so it will need very light and careful handling.

5 To fix a back to the pieces, roll out some clay ¹⁄₆₄in (0.5mm) thick repeating the texture technique—the texture side will be the back. On the smooth side, apply a little water. Gently place the dry section onto the wet clay, then press and hold in place for about one minute. Remove the excess clay using your needle tool. Set to dry.

6 Once fully dried, clean and refine around the edges of the earring pieces. Using foam-backed emery paper and emery boards, work until the two layers are no longer visible. Each earring should look like one seamless piece. Drill a ¹⁄₈in (2mm) hole in the center of the fan shape for the jumpring to go through.

7 Fire the pieces using your preferred method, following the manufacturer's instructions (see page 22). When cooled, brush the metal with a brass brush, and oxidize the earring pieces using liver of sulfur (see page 25), then use a soft cloth and polish. Leave the recess of the design with the heavy patina color. This provides the background color for the polymer inlay.

8 Use polymer clay canes, or mix up some colored polymer clays to create a similar effect. Slice these up and back onto some scrap polymer clay. Pass through a pasta machine on the thinnest setting to create a wafer thin sheet of polymer. Bake the polymer at about 250°F (120°C) for 15 minutes. Let cool.

9 Use a sharp craft knife to slice the baked clay into micro mosaic pieces. Pick up the mosaic piece with the point of the knife, dip each piece in a little PVA glue, then stick pieces into the reservoirs of the design. Let the glue dry and then apply a little resin to fill the remaining spaces.

Ring

YOU WILL NEED

10g Art Clay silver

Art Clay silver paste

1 x fine silver (or silver clay) ring blank

Scrap from polymer clay sheet

PVA glue

Clear resin

This is made using the template and cutting two arcs back to back. At the dry pre-fired stage, attach to a ring blank with clay paste. Follow the rest of the steps in the main project to make the mosaic.

Lightly lubricate your work surface
and tools with a little Badger balm
or olive oil (not Vaseline).

Perfectly Plaid

Get a modern twist on an old classic with this tartan-inspired necklace by Candy Chappill. Perfect under that crisp, white shirt and complemented by a matching bangle.

FOR THE NECKLACE YOU WILL NEED

Approx. 30g Art Clay copper

173 x 3mm bicone-shaped copper beads

39⅜in (1m) length of nylon-coated beading wire

2 x copper crimp beads

2 x 6mm jumprings

1 x copper clasp

Roller

1mm spacer bars

Clay shape template

Needle tool

Small paintbrush

Badger balm or olive oil

Round object (drill bit, mini straw)

Emery paper (foam-backed)

Needle files

Handheld gas torch or kiln

Steel container and carbon (if kiln firing)

Brass brush

Chain-nose pliers

Necklace

1 Roll out the clay ⅟₃₂in (1mm) thick (see page 20). Use your clay template and a needle tool to trace the design, but leave a small tail of clay at the top of your diamond.

2 While the clay is still wet, wrap the tail over a small round object such as a drill bit, and join the end to the main part using a small paintbrush with a tiny amount of water on it. Push the two ends of clay together to make a good join. Make sure that you use plenty of balm on your drill bit. Don't forget the clay shrinks when it dries, so this will help you remove it later.

3 Repeat Steps 1 and 2 a couple of times, but for a smaller design. You want to end up with two smaller ones and one larger one.

4 Once dry, very carefully refine any rough areas using a sanding pad and some needle files. Be careful because it will be very fragile at this stage.

5 Fire your pieces according to the manufacturer's instructions. These pieces were fired in a kiln at 1,778°F (970°C) for 30 minutes (see page 23). Finish them with a brass brush.

6 To assemble your necklace, take the beading wire and cut into two equal pieces to make a necklace about 22in (56cm) in length. Thread a crimp bead onto both pieces, add a jumpring, and loop both wires back through the crimp. Pull tight until the jumpring is sitting up against the crimp. Squash closed with the chain-nose pliers. Thread 30 copper bicone beads onto both wires, then separate the wires and thread 23 copper bicone beads onto one wire. Add one small copper shape, 5 copper beads, the large copper shape, 5 more copper beads, and then the last small copper shape. Now add 23 more copper bicone beads. On the other strand thread on 57 bicone beads. Now bring the two wires together again and thread on 30 more bicones. Thread on the other crimp bead and add the jumpring, pull tight, and squash the crimp bead. Open the jumpring (see page 26), add the clasp, and then close the ring to complete the necklace. Adjust the amount of beads to make the necklace longer or shorter.

When firing Art Clay copper, place the piece on the kiln shelf and sprinkle a light coat of activated coconut carbon over it to minimize firescale.

Once fired, use a nylon-tipped hammer to flatten your pieces if needed. This gives them a crisp look.

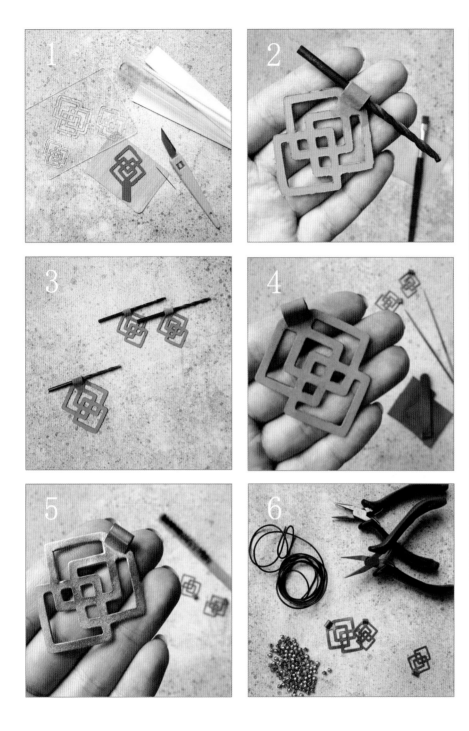

Bangle

YOU WILL NEED

5g Art Clay copper

5 x 6mm copper jumprings

3 x fine wire bangles

Clay-saving templates come in many different designs, shapes, and sizes, so the possibilities are truly endless. Use one for a focal pendant on a set of bangles. Follow the main steps to make the pendant piece, and then attach it to three fine wire bangles using five 6mm copper jumprings (see page 26).

When making up the necklace, crimping pliers make a nicer finish on crimp beads and are widely available.

Italian
Inspiration

Create your own Italian masterpiece with versatile ceramic and PMC clay. Joan Gordon has based this design on some of the elaborately decorated and beautifully ornate buildings in Florence's piazzas.

FOR THE EARRINGS YOU WILL NEED

Dry PMC3 waste clay

Ceramic bisque fired hearts

2 x earring findings

Pestle and mortar

Spray bottle and distilled water

Rubber-tipped shaping tool

Badger balm or olive oil

Plastic sheet (from an old A4 plastic file folder)

Acrylic roller

Empty paste pot

Cocktail stick

Laminated work sheet

Sable paintbrush

Fiber blanket

Brass brush

Agate burnisher

Metal scraper

Rubber block

Liver of sulfur gel

Polishing cloth

Two-part epoxy glue

Paint on the paste and then rub it off the raised areas so that the white clay will contrast with the silver.

Earrings

1 Gather together all your scraps of dried out clay. It can be from clay pots, failed projects, or clay that has been left open for too long. Place it into a mortar and crush, using a circular motion with your hand on the pestle. It will take some time to pulverize it so be patient. This reconstructed clay won't be as strong as fresh clay but it can be used for all sorts of jewelry projects.

2 Fill a spray bottle with distilled water. Spray the clay dust with a small amount of water and mix it slowly using a rubber-tipped shaping tool. Be sparing with the water, as you don't want the clay too wet. Ideally, you are working it until it just pulls together. Leave it for a few minutes so that it firms slightly and then scrape it up and place it on a plastic sheet.

3 Rub a very tiny amount of Badger balm onto two more plastic sheets and onto the palms of your hands. Place the wet clay onto one sheet and cover it with the second. Use your acrylic roller to roll and flatten the clay. Scrape it up, roll it into a ball in your hands, and then roll it between the plastic sheets once more. Do this two or three times until your clay is lovely and smooth.

4 Roll the clay into a ball and place it into a clean, empty clay paste pot. Spray it with two sprays of distilled water and mix this in with the shaping tool. Continue to spray and mix until the clay takes on a smooth, paste-like texture. Place the lid on top of the pot and leave upside-down for an hour. Give it a good stir with a cocktail stick before painting the ceramic hearts.

5 Place the ceramic hearts on a laminated work sheet. Make sure your fingers are grease-free. Dip a sable brush into the paste and paint the front, sides, and back of the heart. Work the brushstrokes in the same direction. When working on the raised relief, dab the brush in and around the design to ensure the paste evenly coats the ceramic. Leave each piece to dry before applying the next coat. Five layers should be enough.

6 Turn the kiln on to a slow setting. Place the hearts onto a fiber blanket and position them into the middle of the kiln. Set the temperature to 1,328°F (720°C) with a hold for 30 minutes (see page 23). Allow the kiln to cool naturally; the ceramic may crack if it is cooled too quickly.

7 Brush the hearts with a soft brass brush and then carefully burnish them with an agate burnisher. The ceramic base isn't strong like metal so take it easy during the burnishing stage.

8 Once polished, if you wish to add a patina, fill a cup with hot water. Dip a paintbrush into the liver of sulfur, then into the hot water, and then paint the surface of each heart. Rinse off any LOS from the heart surface under a faucet of cold running water. Rub off any unwanted patina with a silver polishing cloth.

9 To add the earring backs to the hearts, make up a small amount of glue using two-part epoxy glue. Mix the glue until both parts are completely blended. Dip a cocktail stick into the glue, dab it onto the disc on the earring backing, and then press the earring finding onto the back of a heart. Repeat for the second earring. Let the glue set.

Pendant

YOU WILL NEED

1 x ceramic bisque fired heart

1 x Sterling silver bail

1 x necklace

Coat a heart in the silver paste and make a pendant following the steps in the main project. Once polished, glue a Sterling silver bail to the back and then hang the heart from your choice of necklace.

You could use different-shaped ceramic pieces and glue cufflink findings to the back.

Triangle Trends

Jade Cameron uses beautiful and bespoke textures combined with colorful patinas to create unique chunky copper jewelry that really stands out.

FOR THE EARRINGS YOU WILL NEED

50g Art Clay copper

2 x copper jumprings

2 x niobium copper earwires

3mm spacer bars

Acrylic roller

Rubber texture sheet

CoolSlip Anti-stick spray

¾in (20mm) triangle cutter

Badger balm

2.5mm drill bit and pin vise

Sanding sponges

Brass brush or stainless steel brush

Liver of sulfur

3M polishing papers

Pliers

Earrings

1 Place the 3mm spacers either side of your work surface and roll out your clay (see page 20). Spray a light mist of CoolSlip onto your texture sheet, and lay this on top of the clay. Gently roll over the texture sheet to transfer the texture to the clay. Do not apply too much forward pressure, as you do not want to distort your texture. Peel the texture sheet off to reveal the design. If it has not taken well, roll up the clay and try again.

2 Take your cutter and apply some Badger balm to it. This will give you a smooth cut and will stop the cutter and clay from sticking. Cut two shapes and remove, storing any excess clay in an airtight container. While the clay is still wet try not to handle it too much as it may distort the shape, but if you see any imperfections now is a good time to smooth them out. Let your clay dry—air dry for 24 hours, on a hotplate, or in an oven at 300°F (150°C) for approx. 10 minutes. Make sure your piece is completely dry.

3 When the piece is dry you can drill the holes for the earwire to go through. Take a pin vise and a 2.5mm drill bit and hold the pin vise completely vertical to the piece. Rest the head of the vise in the palm of your hand to keep the drill steady. Turn the drill with your fingers, until you have drilled all the way through. Be gentle; applying too much pressure at this stage may crack your piece.

4 Refine the pieces. This is important, as this is the easiest time to get rid of any imperfections and sharp corners. Use sanding sponges to gently sand the sides, making sure you don't sand away any of the texture. Don't forget the back of the piece. You may only need to use the softer grits.

5 Lay the clay pieces on a kiln shelf and cover with a little charcoal. Fire the pieces in the center of a preheated kiln at 1,778°F (970°C) and hold for 30 minutes, following the manufacturer's instructions (see page 23). Once the pieces are fired, safely remove them from the kiln and quench (see page 23) in cold water immediately. Brush with a brass brush or, if you have any firescale, try using a stainless steel brush.

6 Take the brushed piece and drop it into some warm water with a couple of drops of liver of sulfur; it will turn black almost immediately. Once you have got the depth of patina you want, take the piece out, rinse, and dry. You can now brush or polish the piece to the preferred shine, leaving a lovely dark patina in the grooves of the texture (see page 25). With pliers, add a jumpring through the pre-made hole and attach the earwires (see pages 26 and 29).

For matching pairs of earrings, use the same section of your texture mat to create a more uniform look.

When carving, if you do not apply enough pressure your carving tool can skim across the mat and ruin your design.

Pendant

YOU WILL NEED

50g Art Clay copper

1 x copper pendant bail

Two-part epoxy glue

1 x chunky chain necklace

Make a template for the size you wish to make your pendant. Then follow the main steps, but don't drill a hole in this piece. When fired and finished, glue a pendant bail to the back with glue. Add the bail to a finished chain.

If your rubber mat is too tough to work with, you can warm it slightly and this will make it softer and easier to carve.

Twisted Rope

This opulent stone-set twisted design by Julia Rai looks fabulous as a ring, earrings, or a charm.

FOR THE RING
YOU WILL NEED

15g PMC Flex

Silver metal clay paste or syringe

1 x 5mm cubic zirconia

Ring sizer

Ring mandrel and stand

Teflon or other nonstick work sheet or parchment paper

Sticky tape

Tape measure

Extruder

1mm extruder dye

Sharp craft knife

Good quality paintbrush

Rubber-tipped clay shaper

Fiber blanket

Tumble polisher

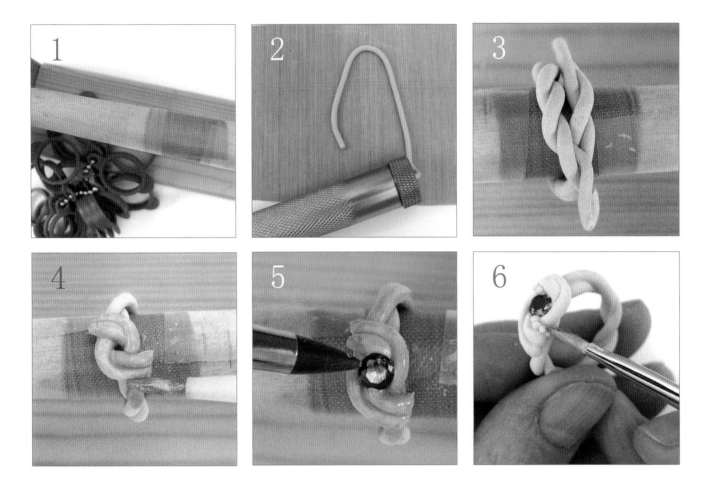

Ring

1 Measure your finger with a ring sizer, then add two sizes to allow for metal clay shrinkage. Slide the ring sizer onto the mandrel and draw a line on each side of the size guide. Wrap parchment paper or a Teflon sheet around the mandrel over the pencil lines and secure it with sticky tape. You will build your ring on this so that it doesn't stick to the mandrel.

2 Use a tape measure to measure the length of the ring from the mandrel. Select a dye for the extruder that has a hole ¹⁄₃₂in (1mm) in diameter. Oil the inside of the extruder barrel and the dye. Form the PMC Flex into a fat sausage and load this into the extruder barrel. Screw on the dye and extrude a snake of clay twice the length of the ring measurement.

3 Extrude another snake the same length as your first snake. Hold both ends of the snakes and twist them together so they form a neat and evenly twisted rope. Carefully form the rope around the mandrel, making sure it is snug underneath. Be careful not to flatten the rope as you do this. The rope should overlap at the top of the mandrel and lie alongside the shank.

4 Curl the ends of the rope around each other at the top of the ring to form a loose bezel for the stone. Cut off the ends at an appropriate length using a sharp craft knife. Use a damp paintbrush to smooth the ends and ensure they are making good contact with the shank of the ring and each other. Check the shank to make sure it's stuck together.

5 While the clay is still wet and pliable, place the stone into the opening at the top of the ring. Use a rubber-tipped clay shaper to push the stone down into the clay, making sure the stone is well embedded. For the clay to grip the stone during firing, the stone table should be flush with the top of the clay bezel. Dry the ring on the mandrel.

6 While the ring is drying, form some tiny metal clay balls for embellishment. Set these aside to dry. Remove the dry ring from the mandrel and use a small amount of paste or syringe to set the ball embellishments around the stone. Clean up as necessary with a damp paintbrush and allow the ring to dry. Clean any paste and dust off the stone, and then fire at 1,652°F (900°C) for two hours (see page 23). Polish with a tumble polisher.

Earrings

YOU WILL NEED

5g PMC Flex

Silver metal clay paste

2 x embeddable eyelets

2 x earwires

Make a pair of twisted rope earrings using the same method as the ring. Simply extrude thinner snakes and push an embeddable eyelet into the top before the clay dries. Roll two tiny balls and stick them to the bottom of the twisted rope. Dry and fire the clay. Add earwires to the eyelets when cooled.

Charm

YOU WILL NEED

5g PMC Flex

Silver metal clay paste

1 x charm bracelet with large links

1 x 6mm jumpring

You can also make a cute little charm using the same method. Extrude a long length of clay and twist into a rope as in Step 3. Let dry a little, and then tie into a knot leaving a space so it's still in a ring shape. Fire, and attach to the bracelet with a jumpring (see page 26).

If you prefer, the ring shank can be two straight lines of clay and not twisted.

This ring would look lovely with a row of smaller stones around the ring shank.

Stylish Hoops

This hoop design is inspired by simple yet ornate patterns from Asia and beyond. Designed by Candy Chappill, these earrings and pendant can easily suit every taste by experimenting with different textures and sizes.

FOR THE EARRINGS YOU WILL NEED

15g Art Clay silver

14 x 6mm jumprings

14 x 5 or 6mm daisy spacer charms

2 x earwires

Roller

1mm spacer bars

Texture tile "Starburst" (Embossed)

CoolSlip Anti-Stick spray

2in (5cm) round cutter

Rounded light bulb

1in (2.5cm) round cutter

Emery paper (foam-backed)
or baby wipe

2mm drill bit and pin vise

Brass brush

Liver of sulfur (optional)

Polishing papers

Chain-nose pliers

Flat-nose pliers

Earrings

1 Roll out your clay ½₃₂in (1mm) thick (see page 20) on top of the texture tile. Cut out your first shape using the 2in (5cm) round cutter. Use the CoolSlip Anti-Stick spray on your cutter edge and texture tile in particular, to stop your clay sticking.

2 Add some of the spray to the light bulb. Place your round piece of textured clay onto the light bulb. Use the 1in (2.5cm) round cutter to cut out your second shape, slightly off center. Let dry. It's easier to cut this second shape on the light bulb, to save misshaping your piece when trying to move it.

3 Once dry, refine with a sanding pad. This stage can be very tricky as it's a hollow shape and only ½₃₂in (1mm) thick, so it will be very fragile. If it doesn't need much sanding, you could always run a baby wipe over the surface to smooth it off nicely.

4 Drill a hole in the smallest part of the earring using the 2mm drill bit (see page 21). This hole is for your earwire so try and make it as central as possible. Continue to drill seven more ⅛in (2mm) holes around the edge of the bottom of the hoop.

5 Once all your holes are drilled and your piece is completely dry, fire in a kiln for half an hour at 1,472°F (800°C) (see page 23). Once fired, use a brass brush and then oxidize with liver of sulfur if desired (see page 25). Use polishing papers to create a shine on the silver if desired.

6 Once all polished, you can attach your daisy spacer charms, by hanging them straight onto the jumprings (see page 26). Attach the earwires.

When drilling your seven charm holes, it's easier to mark the back with a pen so they will look much more even.

You can alter the design slightly by choosing another texture or making them smaller or larger.

Pendant

YOU WILL NEED

7g Art Clay silver

7 x 6mm jumprings

7 x 5 or 6mm daisy spacer charms

1 x leather thong necklace

This would look great a little larger and as a statement pendant. Follow the main project steps to make the silver hoop shape and add daisy spacer charms. Don't drill the earring hole in Step 4, and instead simply use a gorgeous leather thong to hang it off by tying a larks head knot. You could even try making your own little charms to hang off the bottom. Make it a keepsake pendant with special mementos.

This texture tile is just asking to be filled with color. Imagine each little sun shape being filled with a different color.

Rainbow Wraps

This appliqué technique developed by Leigh Armstrong can create stunning results with little effort or need for expensive tools. Try making your own texture mats from items such as leaves or lace to create something unique.

FOR THE BRACELET YOU WILL NEED

9g PMC3

PMC3 syringe or paste

Ribbon

Two-part molding compound

Roller

Playing cards

Badger balm or olive oil

Texture mat

Cutter

Cocktail straw

2000-grit sandpaper

Nail file

Needle tool or cocktail stick

Paintbrush

Handheld gas torch

Firebrick

Stainless steel brush

Burnisher

Polishing papers or tumble polisher

Silver polish

Liver of sulfur (optional)

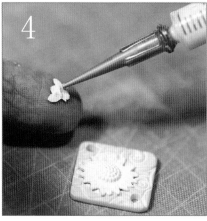

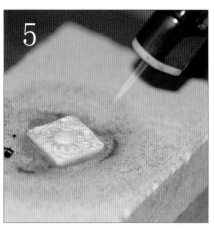

Care should be taken as some molding compounds can leave a slightly oily residue, so be very careful if you are attempting to mold porous or delicate items.

Pendant

YOU WILL NEED

5g PMC3

PMC3 syringe or paste

1 x 6mm jumpring

1 x ready-made chain

You can use the same techniques to create a matching pendant. After you have created the shape in Step 2 and refined it, only cut one hole in the place where you want the pendant to hang. Continue to follow the steps to finish the piece. When fired, add a jumpring to the hole (see page 26) and hang from a ready-made chain.

Bracelet

1 Using a two-part molding compound, mold any small items that interest you, e.g. tiny seashells, old earrings, buttons, or anything else that is no bigger than ⅝in (1.5cm) (see page 24). Once your mold is solid to the touch, fill with metal clay. Remove excess by gently rubbing your thumb from the center to the edge until you can see the outline properly and have created a flat back to the molded clay.

2 To create your wrist-wrap base, roll out your clay to five cards thick (⅛in/2mm) (see page 20). Apply your rolled clay to a lightly oiled texture mat such as "Swirly Q" by Lisa Pavelka. Choose a cutter and cut your clay to shape, e.g. a simple square. Once cut, use a thin cocktail drinking straw to cut two holes opposite one another ready to thread your ribbon through (see page 21).

3 Once your base piece has thoroughly dried out, use a high-grade grit piece of sandpaper to smooth the edges. If you have chosen to do a square you need to soften the corners so that it will be comfortable to wear. Do this by gently sanding off the corner points using a nail file.

4 Remove your dried pieces from the molds and, using a needle tool or cocktail stick, gently remove any "tags" of clay around the edges. Using either syringe or paste clay, attach the moldings to the wrist-wrap base, pressing firmly to ensure a good joint and using a damp paintbrush to remove any excess syringe or paste. Let it dry again.

5 Place the piece onto a firebrick and fire using a gas torch. Gently move the torch flame over the entire piece, allowing the organic binder to burn away. Once the silver has reached an apricot color, continue to gently move the flame over the piece for at least three minutes. Remove the flame and carefully quench in cold water (see page 22).

6 Use a soft steel brush to bring a shine to the silver. Next use a burnisher, then either tumble the silver or use polishing papers, working from the rough grade through to the fine. Once polished you can either leave as it is or, using liver of sulfur, patina it (see page 25). Thread through a ribbon of your choice, long enough to wrap around your wrist at least twice. Secure with a knot or bow.

Hollywood Glamour

With a contemporary twist on a vintage classic, Tracey Spurgin has turned this focal silver bow into a pendant with a unique lace texture. Decorate with crystals and pearls.

FOR THE PENDANT YOU WILL NEED

20g Art Clay silver

A little paste or syringe

1 x embeddable eyelet

48 x 8mm faceted turquoise glass beads

73 x 2.5mm (size 8) silver seed beads

2 x 12mm faceted turquoise glass beads

1 x large faceted turquoise glass teardrop pendant

18 x 2in (50mm) silver-colored eyepins

1 x 2in (50mm) silver-colored headpin

4 x 6mm jumprings

1 x clasp

Paper pattern

Badger balm or olive oil

Roller

1.5mm spacer bars

1mm spacer bars

Lace texture

Needle tool or craft knife

Pieces of plastic straw

Needle files

Emery paper (foam-backed)

1.5mm drill bit and pin vise

Polishing papers

Brass brush or radial disc on a rotary tool

Pendant

1 The paper pattern provided can be traced or photocopied to enlarge the scale of your project. Carefully cut out the paper pattern and generously apply Badger balm or olive oil.

2 Prepare the work surface, and then roll out 20g of clay, using 1.5mm spacers (see page 20). Lay the clay on some lace, and then place 1mm spacers on top with a second piece of lace. Firmly roll over the lace once only.

3 Remove the lace and place the paper pattern onto the clay. The Badger balm will help the paper stick to the clay while you cut around the outline with a craft knife or needle tool. Remove the excess clay.

4 Place the piece with the right side of your texture facing down. Lay two pieces of plastic straw along the widest point of the bow, and gently lift the side to make the ends meet in the middle. Set aside while you repeat the texture process to cut out the two bow tails. Dry all the parts.

5 Remove the straws from the bow, then file and refine all the edges of all pieces with sanding paper. Be careful to support the bow at the center at all times. The weight of the wide ends could be enough to fracture the clay under its own weight.

6 Attach the bow tails to the main body of the bow. One end squeezes into the inside of the bow, while the second piece is adhered to the back of the bow. Use a little paste or syringe to join the pieces together. Set aside to dry once more.

7 To make the knot of the bow, roll out and texture the clay once again. Cut a piece approx. ⅜in (10mm) wide. The clay is deliberately distorted with a straw at this point to give the knot a more authentic look. Wrap around the middle of the bow, making a join at the back.

8 Insert an eyelet into the lower end of the bow knot. Set the piece aside to dry once more. Use the file to refine all edges and parts. Drill a hole in each end to take jumprings, for hanging the piece from a necklace.

9 Fire the bow in the usual manner. This piece was kiln-fired at 1,472°F (800°C) for 20 minutes (see page 23). Once fired, polish. This can be done with a handheld brass brush or using a brass brush disc with a rotary tool. To make this piece into a necklace, either add to a plain chain using jumprings to attach the bow or make a chain of beaded components using the technique for simple loops (see page 27) to make the beaded pieces. If making a beaded chain, use eyepins instead of headpins and then follow the technique, placing three faceted beads on each eyepin with a silver seed bead in between. Make two chains of eight beaded components (see page 29) with three 8mm beads and one 12mm bead on each. Add a jumpring to either end on both chains. Attach one end of each chain to the holes cut in the bow using the jumprings already attached to the chains (see page 26). Add a clasp at the end on one chain and add a final beaded end piece using the large teardrop-shape bead with three silver seed beads underneath and two above strung on a headpin.

Template
Printed at 95%.
Reduce or enlarge to make the project at the size you want.

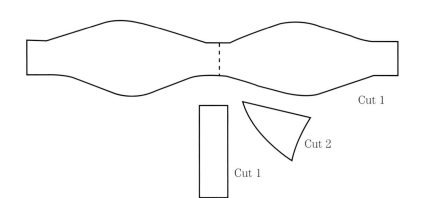

Cut 1

Cut 2

Cut 1

Have a clear design in mind. If necessary, try out your ideas (such as rolling the pattern) in polymer clay first.

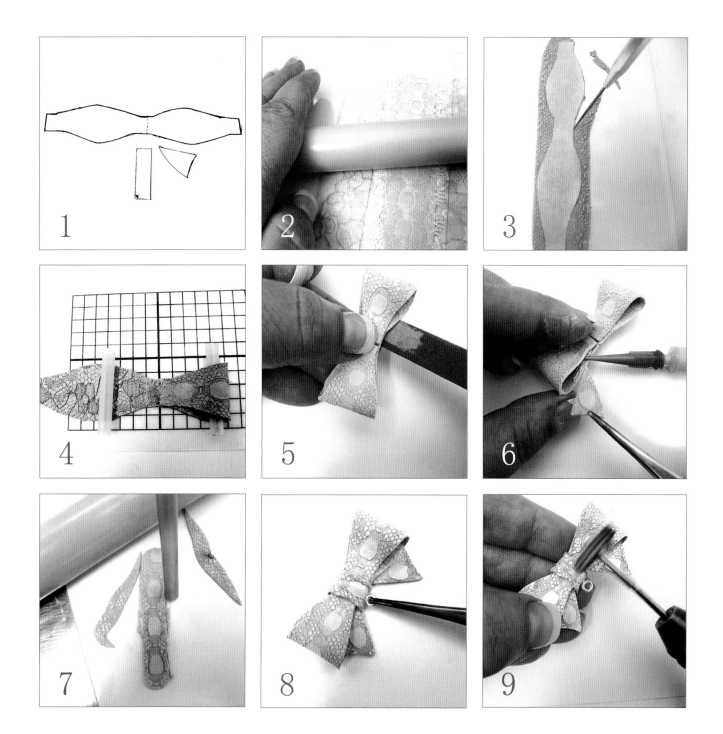

Don't forget to prepare the clay after opening by rolling it fast and hard in the heel of your hands. Bring the clay to a soft putty ball, with no cracks or fold lines.

Spirit of Egypt

The metal clay focal panel in this bracelet by Julia Rai features the Egyptian symbol for protection and health, the Eye of Ra. It's complemented by semiprecious beads, with matching earrings and pendant to make too.

FOR THE BRACELET YOU WILL NEED

10g Art Clay silver

Art Clay silver paste

1 x 3mm kiln-safe cubic zirconia (CZ)

12 x 1½in (38mm) silver eyepins

8 x 6mm jumprings

4mm jade beads

6mm jasper beads

Carnelian nuggets

1 x silver-plated box clasp

Egyptian-themed push mold

Small paintbrush

Roller

Teflon or other nonstick sheet

Tissue blade or sharp craft knife

Playing cards

Small round nesting cutters

Sanding pads/papers/emery board

3–3.5mm drill bit and pin vise

Tumble polisher or brass/steel brush

Liver of sulfur and polishing papers (optional)

Round-nose pliers and cutters

Bead board

Earrings

YOU WILL NEED

10g silver metal clay

Thick silver clay paste

2 x embeddable fine silver eyelets

2 x turquoise donuts

2 x 8mm jasper beads

2 x 2in (50mm) silver-colored eyepins

2 x earwires

Mold two small Egyptian lotus motifs in silver clay, embedding the eyelets at the top. Thread turquoise donuts with a jasper bead in the middle onto the silver eyepins and make a simple loop on the end (see page 27). Attach the motifs to one end (see page 29) and the earwires to the other end to finish the earrings.

Bracelet

1   Oil the mold well using a paintbrush to get into all areas of the design. Pinch off a little clay and wrap up for later. Roll the remaining clay into a smooth ball and push this well down into the mold. Smooth the surface with a damp finger and then carefully pop it out of the mold onto the Teflon sheet and trim the edges with a tissue blade.

2   Take the remaining clay and roll it out three cards thick. Using round nesting cutters, cut donuts and then cut them in half using your tissue blade. Let these dry. Let the molded panel dry completely then use a sanding stick to refine the back and edges if necessary. Use thick paste to attach the dried half-donuts to the sides of the molded panel to form loops.

3   Drill a dip in the molded panel where you want to put the cubic zirconia (CZ), supporting the panel from behind. Keep checking your CZ in the dip to make sure it fits. The CZ should sit well down in the dip, so when you look across the surface of the panel, you shouldn't see any of the stone above the surface. Dampen the hole lightly, add paste, and push the CZ in.

4   When the panel is completely dry, check that the CZ is firmly embedded, remove any trace of paste from the surface of the stone, and fire (see page 23). If you're using a kiln, fire at 1,472°F (800°C) for two hours. Air cool, brush the piece, and tumble polish. An option is to oxidize the panel using liver of sulfur (see page 25) and use polishing papers to shine up the high spots of the design.

5   Take some time to plan out your bead design using a bead board or mat. Group two or three beads per eyepin and make sure you leave enough of the eyepin protruding to form a loop. Attach two eyepins to each side of the panel using jumprings (see page 26). Thread on the beads and, using round-nose pliers, form a loop on the end of each eyepin (see page 27).

6   Create more eyepin bead segments with a loop at each end until you have enough for the size you need. Use three segments with three beads on each. Attach these segments to each other using jumprings and then attach the silver-plated box clasp parts to each end, ensuring they're the right way up. Try the bracelet on to make sure it fits and adjust if necessary.

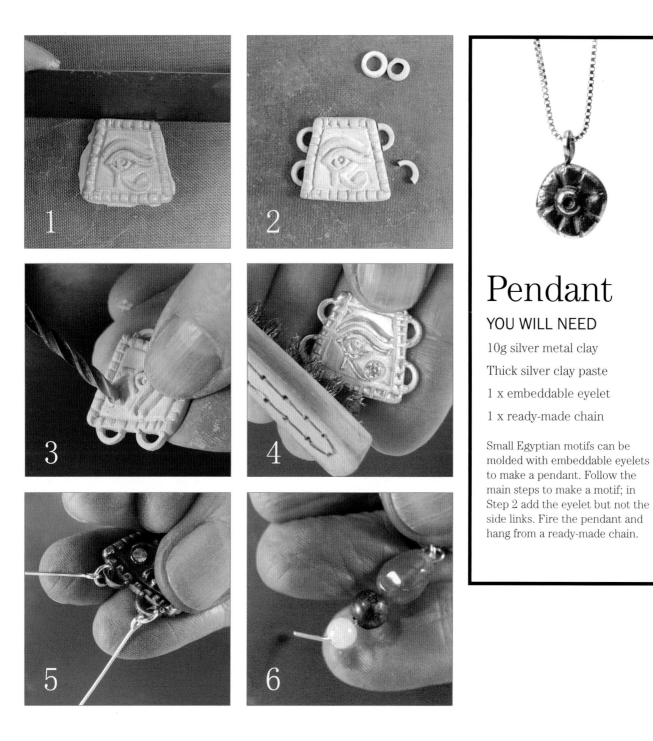

Pendant

YOU WILL NEED

10g silver metal clay

Thick silver clay paste

1 x embeddable eyelet

1 x ready-made chain

Small Egyptian motifs can be molded with embeddable eyelets to make a pendant. Follow the main steps to make a motif; in Step 2 add the eyelet but not the side links. Fire the pendant and hang from a ready-made chain.

Use your favourite button, or something else, and make your own mold.

Fly a Kite

Revive your childhood memories of kite flying with this jaunty design by Sandra Quell.

FOR THE NECKLACE YOU WILL NEED

10g Art Clay silver

Art Clay silver paste or syringe

22 x 4mm Swarovski crystals

3 x Sterling silver headpins

3 x Sterling silver eyepins

22 x 4mm bicone crystals

Beading wire

3–4mm string of freshwater pearls

2 x crimp beads

2 x crimp covers

1 x Sterling silver clasp

Tracing paper or thin paper

Scratch-Foam (very thin polystyrene sheet)

Sticky tape

Ballpoint pen

Roller

Playing cards or spacer bars

Needle tool

Cocktail stick

Baby wipes

1.2mm drill bit and pin vise

Paintbrush

Brass brush

Burnisher

2 pairs of flat-nose pliers

Crimp pliers

Wire cutter

Pendant

YOU WILL NEED

10g Art Clay silver

3 x Sterling silver headpins

3 x Sterling silver eyepins

6 x 4mm bicone crystals

Ready-made snake chain

Make the kite following the main steps. At Step 2 make one bail big enough to allow the end of a snake chain to go through it (don't forget that the bail will shrink). Attach the bail at the center top on the back. When fired and polished, thread the chain through the bail and add the beaded pieces (from Step 6) to finish.

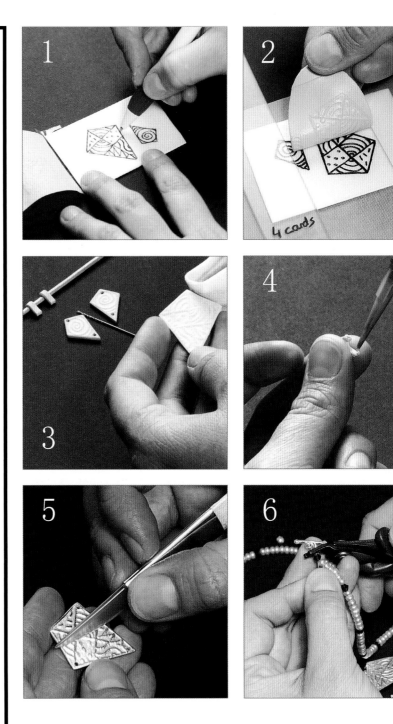

Choose Swarovski crystals in different colors to make a multicolored necklace.

Use fancy headpins and a delicate texture to give your kite a more graceful appearance.

Necklace

1 To make the texture plate, draw your design onto tracing paper or onto another type of thin paper and lay it on top of a sheet of Scratch-Foam. Fix it with sticky tape. Trace the design with a ballpoint pen. Remove the tracing paper and deepen the lines on the Scratch-Foam by gently going over them with the pen.

2 Roll the clay six cards thick or use 2mm spacer bars (see page 20). Lay it onto the Scratch-Foam sheet and roll it to a thickness of four cards or $\frac{1}{16}$in (1.5mm). Peel away your textured clay and turn it over. Cut out your kite with a needle tool and let it dry. Make two small bails by placing two ribbons of clay (four cards thick) over a cocktail stick.

3 The bails can be tiny as they will only have beading wire running through them. Refine the edges and the back of your kite and your bails with a baby wipe and let them dry. Drill holes at the bottom and at the corners of the kite (see page 21). Mark the place for the bails with a pencil. Place them at different heights so the kite flies diagonally upward.

4 Put a little water where you want your bails to go and let it soak into the clay. Add some paste or syringe to the ends of the bails and press them onto your pencil marks. Clean up the paste or syringe around the bails with a damp brush by pushing it into the gaps under the bails. Let your piece dry completely and fire for two hours at 1,652°F (900°C) (see page 23).

5 Brush the kite with a brass brush and polish the raised parts of your texture with a burnisher. Thread three crystals onto headpins, form loops (see page 27), and attach two of them to the corner holes of the kite (see page 29). Thread three crystals onto eyepins, make loops, and form a chain dangling from the bottom hole of the kite. End the chain with the third crystal on a headpin.

6 String your kite onto the beading wire. String a series of nine pearls alternating with one crystal onto the beading wire on both sides of the kite, until the necklace reaches your desired length. Thread crimp beads onto both ends and use crimp pliers to close them. Attach the clasp to one end with a jumpring (see page 26).

Give the kite a liver of sulfur treatment and polish the raised parts of your design to make the lines stand out.

Earrings

YOU WILL NEED

10g Art Clay silver

2 x Sterling silver headpins

2 x 4mm Swarovski crystals

2 x 4mm bicone crystals

2 x earwires

Make smaller kites to hang onto earwires. Make a smaller Scratch-Foam texture for the earrings, and then follow the steps to make the silver kites. These need holes at the top and bottom but don't drill the side corners. Once fired and polished, thread the top holes onto earwires and add a beaded end piece (see page 29) to the bottoms.

Maltese Magic

This design by Tracey Spurgin is based on the 15th-century Maltese cross that features two points on each of the four arms. Make earrings to match this dynamic pendant.

FOR THE PENDANT YOU WILL NEED

20g Art Clay silver

Art Clay silver paste

12in (30.5cm) length of US 20-gauge (SWG 21, 0.8mm) wire

Two-part molding compound

1 x 4mm round pearl

1 x rolo chain

5 x 5mm Sterling silver jumprings

Graph paper and laminated graph paper

Cocktail sticks

Badger balm or olive oil

Roller

1mm spacer bars

Craft knife

Circle template or cookie cutter

Needle tool

Files

Sanding papers

Snake roller

Tissue blade

Polishing papers

Tumble polisher or radial disc on a rotary drill

Liver of sulfur

Polish and soft cloth

Pliers and wire cutters

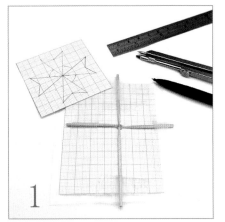

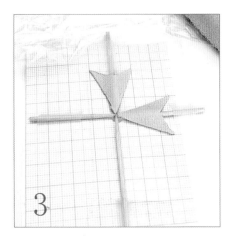

Pendant

1 Begin by drafting out the pattern on graph paper to achieve the geometric design. Also prepare a second laminated piece of graph paper, with four cocktail sticks taped to it in a cross with the points in the center following the graph lines. Cut out your paper template from one of the four arms of the cross.

2 Prepare a work surface with a little Badger balm. Roll and texture a piece of clay ½in (1mm) thick (see page 20). Lightly balm the paper template, place the template on the clay, and use a craft knife to accurately cut out the clay.

3 Next lift each of the four cut clay arms and place them over the cocktail sticks, ensuring all the points of the arms meet on the center. Reference the graph lines to help maintain symmetry. Place a piece of plastic wrap over the top of the pieces, then use a sponge to lightly press down; this will help the clay "hug" the shape of the stick. Set the pieces aside to dry.

4 Roll out and texture some more clay using the circle cookie cutter or circle template with a needle tool to cut out the backing circle. Once again set this aside to dry.

5 Once all the pieces are dry, refine the edges with a little sanding, using files and papers. Take the pin vise and 1.25mm drill bit and drill a hole to hang the pendant in the outer edge of one arm. Lightly draw a cross onto the backing circle in pencil, using a little paste applied to the back on the point of the arms. Add a little water to the circle, and then join the pieces together. Use the graph once more to reference and maintain the 90-degree angles.

6 Take two lengths of the wire and twist them together. Next mix some two-part molding compound (see page 24), roll it into a snake length, and place over the twisted wire. Let the compound cure, then flex the mold to release the wire.

7 Lightly balm the mold and roll out a piece of silver clay into a snake using a snake roller. Lay the snake of clay onto the mold pressing down firmly, roll over with your regular roller to force the clay into the mold, and remove the excess with a tissue blade. Flex the mold to release the silver clay. Use a rulerto ensure your clay twist lies in a straight line while it dries.

8 Once the clay twists are dry, break them into shorter manageable lengths—they can be attached to the edge of the arms using a little paste and water. Leave to dry, and then refine by filling in any gaps or filing any excess.

9 Fire the piece, either by handheld gas torch, gas hob, or in a kiln on 1,472°F (800°C) for 20 minutes (see page 23). Polish the piece and then patinate with liver of sulfur (see page 25), giving a final polish using a soft cloth and silver polish. To complete the piece, a small pearl has been glued into the center. Attach the pendant to a chain by making a five-link chain with the jumprings and attach one end to the rolo chain and the other through the hole in the pendant (see page 26.)

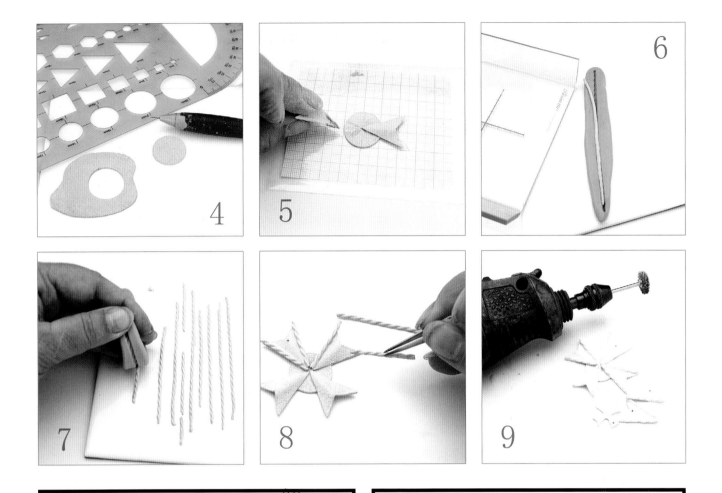

Small pendant

YOU WILL NEED

10g Art Clay silver

1 x 4mm fireable cubic zirconia

1 x 5mm Sterling silver jumpring

1 x rolo chain

Make a simplified or smaller pendant using the same technique for a variation on the main cross design. In Step 1 make a much simpler design and cut the template as one piece. Roll and texture the clay then cut out the design. Push the fireable crystal into the middle so that the crystal is level with the surface of the clay. Drill a hole where you want the top of the pendant to be and let dry. Fire and polish, then patinate with liver of sulfur if desired. Open the jumpring and attach the pendant to a chain (see page 26).

Earrings

YOU WILL NEE D

10g Art Clay silver

1 x 4mm fireable cubic zirconia

1 x 5mm Sterling silver jumpring

1 x rolo chain

Make a simplified or smaller pendant using the same technique for a variation on the main cross design. In Step 1 make a much simpler design and cut the template as one piece. Roll and texture the clay then cut out the design. Push the fireable crystal into the middle so that the crystal is level with the surface of the clay. Drill a hole where you want the top of the pendant to be and leave to dry. Fire and polish, then patinate with liver of sulfur if desired. Open the jumpring and attach the pendant to a chain (see page 26).

Firework Fun

Capture the magic of New Year's Eve fireworks with this sparkling set by Sandra Quell, using the vibrant colors of Swarovski's Vitrail medium crystals.

FOR THE PENDANT YOU WILL NEED

10g Art Clay silver

Art Clay syringe

3 x cubic zirconias (1mm, 2mm, or 5mm)

14mm Swarovski Rivoli (color: Vitrail Medium)

28in (70cm) length of US 24-gauge (SWG 25, 0.5mm) Sterling silver wire

Paper for template

Roller

Playing cards

Needle tool

Paintbrush

Baby wipes

1.5mm drill bit and pin vise

Brass brush

½in (13mm) star-shaped cutter

Liver of sulfur

Polish

Flat-nose pliers and wire cutters

You can adapt the pendant to suit any occasion by replacing the stars with other shapes, changing the texture and the outer form of the ring, and choosing Rivoli in a different color.

Earrings

YOU WILL NEED

5g Art Clay silver

2 x 2mm cubic zirconias

2 x 2in (50mm) Sterling silver eyepins

2 x Sterling silver earwires

2 x 4mm bicone crystals

Make two small stars using Steps 2 and 3 and drill holes in one point on each star. Fire and polish. Take the eyepins and open the loops (see page 29), attaching each one to a star. Add a crystal to each eyepin and make wrapped loops above (see page 28). Before closing the loops, add the earwires.

To choose the drying form for the bail, such as a straw, think about the width of your ring so you get a bail that fits your pendant.

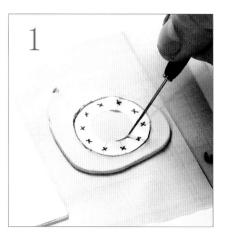

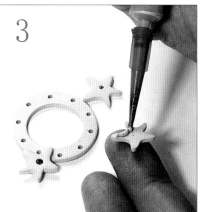

Pendant

1 Create a paper template for the ring (inner diameter: ¾in (18mm), outer diameter: 1³⁄₁₆in (30mm) or more). Choose whatever shape you like for the outer form. Distribute 10 holes evenly around the circle with a distance of 1in (2.5cm) between opposite holes. Cut out the template. Roll out your clay four cards thick (¹⁄₁₆in/1.5mm) (see page 20). Lay your paper template onto the clay and cut around it with a needle tool. Let it dry.

2 When the clay is leather hard, texture it with a wire brush and mark the places of the holes. Let it dry completely. Roll out the clay four cards thick and cut out three little stars and a ¹⁄₁₆ x ³⁄₁₆in (1.5 x 5mm) rectangle for the bail. Press your cubic zirconias into the middle of the stars and let them dry. Place the rectangle over a straw or pencil to dry.

3 Refine the ring with baby wipes and drill ¹⁄₁₆in (1.5mm) holes where you made the marks earlier (see page 21). Refine the stars and the bail as well and join the stars to your ring with a little bit of slip or syringe. Take care not to obscure the holes for the wire. Clean up the joins with a wet brush. Let your piece dry.

4 Join the bail to the back of your ring. Clean up the joins as well. Let your piece dry completely. Fire it in a kiln for two hours at 1,652°F (900°C) or according to the manufacturer's instructions (see page 22). Brush the finished piece with a brass brush. Apply a liver of sulfur patina (see page 25). Polish the stars back to a high shine and give the ring a slight polish as well to highlight the texture.

5 Take a 14in (35cm) length of wire. Pass the wire through hole 1 from the back to the front (1b–f), then through hole 5 front to back (5f–b). Go on weaving the following pattern: 9b–f, 3f–b, 7b–f. Insert the Rivoli and go on weaving 1f–b, 5b–f, 9f–b, 3b–f, 7f–b. Pass the wire back to hole 1 and twist it together with the other end.

6 Take the second length of wire (also 14in/35cm) and weave the following pattern: 2b-f, 6f-b, 10b-f, 4f-b, 8b-f, 2f-b, 6b-f, 10f-b, 4b-f, 8f-b. End the weave at the back of hole 2 by twisting the wire ends together. Cut the twisted wires and bend the ends under a wire so that they don't hurt you when you wear the pendant.

Keep a medium tension in your wire when weaving to keep the Rivoli in place.

Mobile phone charm

YOU WILL NEED

5g Art Clay silver

1 x 2mm cubic zirconia

1 x 2in (50mm) Sterling silver eyepin

Mobile phone connector

3 x 4mm bicone crystals

Make a firework charm for your phone with a little star and bicone crystals. Make the star following Steps 2 and 3 and drill a hole in one point. Fire and polish. Take the eyepin and open the loop (see page 29), attach it to the star. Add the three crystals to the eyepin and make a wrapped loop above the crystals (see page 28). Before closing the loop, add the mobile phone connector.

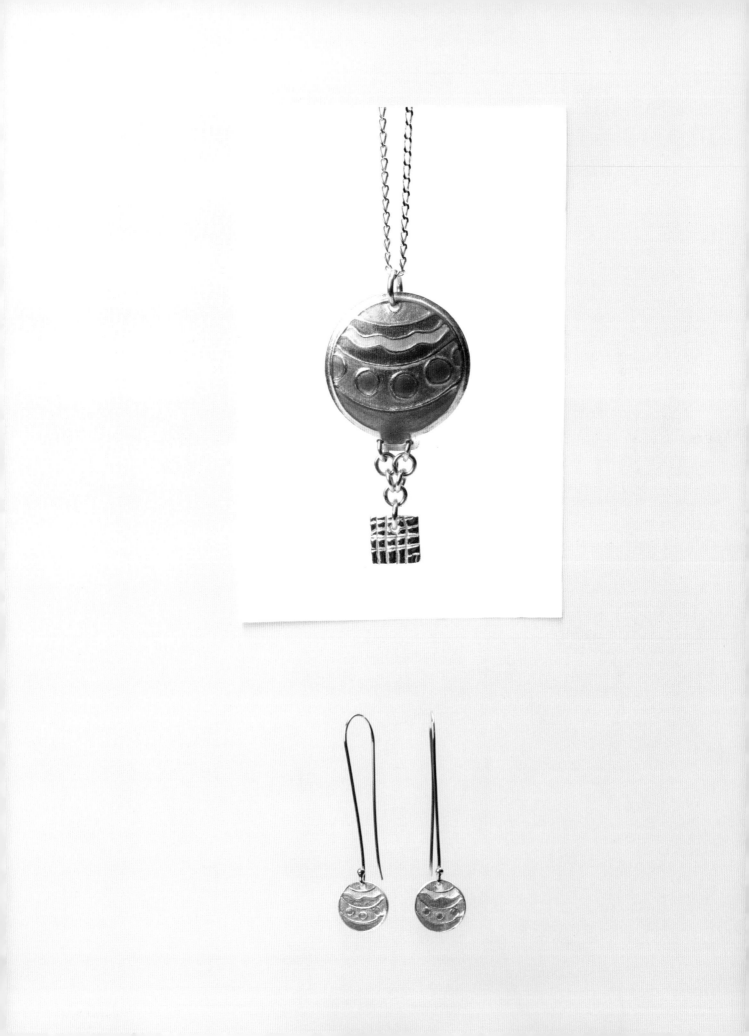

Up and Away

This project by Emma Gordon uses polystyrene to make the texture sheet for the balloon. It is really simple to use and a fantastic way to design your own textures.

FOR THE PENDANT YOU WILL NEED

16g PMC3

9 x 6mm jumprings

1 x chain

Polystyrene (Safeprint A4 foam sheets)

Ball burnisher or ballpoint pen

Roller

Playing cards

Badger balm or olive oil

Square and round cookie cutters or stencils

Needle tool

Measuring spoon

Rubber block

Sandpaper or sanding pads

Drill and bits

Agate burnisher or tumble polisher

UV resin (P2 Jelly)

Mica powder

Aluminum foil

Cocktail sticks

UV lamp

Pliers

Instead of mica powders to color the resin, you can use glass paints or colorants for resin or glitter. Enamel can also be used.

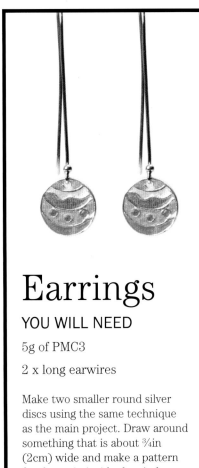

Earrings

YOU WILL NEED

5g of PMC3

2 x long earwires

Make two smaller round silver discs using the same technique as the main project. Draw around something that is about ¾in (2cm) wide and make a pattern for the resin inside the circle. Follow Steps 1 to 3, and make two. At Step 3 you only need to drill one hole at the top on each disc (see page 21). Follow Steps 4 to 6 to color the discs. Then thread them onto the loop on long earwires (see page 29).

Pendant

1 Draw out your design on paper first to test that it works and you are happy with it. Cut a 6 x 6in (15 x 15cm) square of polystyrene from the A4 sheet and draw on your design using a ball burnisher. Use the smallest one you have, or a ballpoint pen if you don't have one. Draw over your design several times, taking care not to push through the polystyrene sheet (see page 22).

2 Roll out your clay to four cards thick and texture the clay (see page 20). Make the basket part of the design by rolling out your clay to four cards thick and applying a basket-like texture (you could use a seed pod for this, as it will have a similar texture). Cut out a square that is an appropriate size for your basket design. Drill a hole.

3 Cut out your balloon shape with a needle tool. Use a circle template larger than the design, and then trim around the bottom part. It leaves a nice border around the edge, which frames the balloon. Put the balloon on the back of a round spoon to give it a slight curve. Set aside to dry. Once your pieces are ready, smooth and tidy the edges with sandpaper, using a rubber block to support the clay. Drill holes for the jumprings, one at the top in the center and two in the square base (see page 21).

4 Fire your clay as normal. Your clay should also be polished, because once the resin is applied, it cannot be polished again. For this project use UV resin and mica powder to add color. Mica powder also has a lovely shimmer. Prepare your work surface, making sure it's clean and dust-free. Mix your resin on aluminum foil for a quick and easy way to clear up afterward.

5 Put a small blob of resin onto the foil and put some mica powder on top. Use a cocktail stick to mix the powder and the resin together. Mix from the bottom to minimize air bubbles. The more powder you put into the resin, the deeper your color will be. Mix each color separately and use a new cocktail stick for each.

6 Put your piece back on the spoon and fix it with polymer clay to hold secure. The surface needs to be as flat as possible to apply the resin properly. Apply each color with a cocktail stick separately because it will be easier to correct any mistakes. If you spill over the lines, wipe with a damp cloth or rinse under warm water. Once the color is applied, cure under a UV light for a minimum of five minutes. Repeat for each color. Finish with jumprings (see page 26) and a chain.

Before curing the resin, agitate your piece and then apply an open flame from a candle or similar. This should pop any air bubbles lying beneath the surface of the resin.

You can use a two-part resin for this design, in place of the UV variety, but it needs a full 24 hours to cure. The UV variety is quicker and less wasteful.

Wintry Wonder

This stunning snowflake design by Tracey Spurgin has a beautiful gem hidden inside.

FOR THE PENDANT YOU WILL NEED

30g Art Clay silver

Art Clay paste or syringe

1 x snake chain

Badger balm or olive oil

Roller

2mm spacer bars

1.5mm spacer bars

QuikArt 54817 Texture Pairs

QuikArt 2 Step Template—Holiday Snowflakes

Needle tool

Circle cutters

Tissue blade

Fireable gemstone

3mm spacer bars

Brass brush

Files

Sanding grits

Polishing papers

Fiber blanket

Tumble polisher or wire brush

Pendant

1 You will need to use products from the QuikArt range for this project: a texture mat and a snowflake template. Prepare all other tools, materials, and equipment. Lightly oil a work surface.

2 Roll out the clay ⅛in (2mm) thick (see page 20). Lay the clay on top of the texture plate. Place 1.5mm spacers on top of the plate, then lay the second plate face down on the clay. As these plates are a positive and negative of the same pattern, use both plates to texture both sides of the clay.

3 Use the snowflake stencil with a needle tool to carefully cut around the outline. Ensure the needle tool is held at 90 degrees to the work surface to achieve clean-cut outlines. For one side of the snowflake, use a circle cutter to cut a hole in the center.

4 Using a tissue blade, carefully lift the cutout clay and drape over a form to create a dome. This wooden dome is the knob handle from a salt pot, but measuring spoons or light bulbs are also useful formers. Be careful when moving wet clay as it's very easy to stretch or distort out of shape. Set this aside to dry. Repeat Steps 1 to 4, this time without the center hole. This second side will create the back of the snowflake. Let dry.

5 To add a gemstone to hide inside, roll out clay ⅛in (3mm) thick. Push a fireable gemstone into the clay by gently rolling over to ensure the stone table is level with the surface of the clay. Place a piece of plastic wrap over the clay then use the circle cutter to cut through the clay. This gives a lovely rounded edge to the clay without the need for filing and sanding. Set aside to dry.

6 Once dry, refine all the edges of the stone setting and the two halves of the snowflake, with files or grits, being careful not to file off the surface texture on the snowflake.

7 Proceed with caution on this step. Sit the snowflake with the edges down on sanding grit. Using contact points to hold the domed snowflake, gently rotate the dry clay in a circle or figure-of-eight. This is to take down the cut edges to taper the edge. The aim here is to make the two halves of the snowflake meet.

8 Use a little paste or syringe to adhere the gemstone setting to the center back inside the cupped half of the snowflake. Next use a little paste or syringe to join the contact points on the two snowflake halves. Let aside to dry once more.

9 To fire the snowflake in the kiln, support the piece with a fiber blanket to ensure the work doesn't slump during firing. Fire at 1,472°F (800°C) for 20 minutes (see page 23). Once fired, wire brush or use a tumble polisher to complete the piece. Thread a snake chain through one point on the snowflake.

Earrings

YOU WILL NEED

10g Art Clay silver

2 x earwires

Make two snowflake shapes, then drill a hole in one point on each snowflake. Dry flat, then refine the edges with sanding grits and fire (see page 23). Brush with a brass brush and water for a satin finish. Hang from a pair of earwires (see page 29).

This project would work with any shape.
Just remember to cut two, and make sure
you dry them on a dome.

Bright Owl

Although this cute owl is pure silver, the different finishes used by Sandra Quell add depth and interest to the design.

FOR THE PIN YOU WILL NEED

10g Art Clay silver

Art Clay syringe

Art Clay paper type approx. ¾ x ¾in (2 x 2cm)

Fireable pin back

A small amount of black polymer clay

Paper for template

Roller

1.5mm spacer bars

Needle tools

Files

Sanding pads or baby wipes

Carving tool

Drill bit and pin vise

Silicone-tipped clay shaper

Brass brush

Handheld electric rotary tool

Tumble polisher (optional to polish if not using a rotary tool)

Liver of sulfur

3M radial bristle discs for the rotary tool

Silicon tip for the rotary tool

Burnisher

Pumice powder

Two-part epoxy glue

Earrings

YOU WILL NEED

10g Art Clay silver

Art Clay paper type approx.
¾ x ¾in (2 x 2cm)

Art Clay syringe

2 x ear posts with flat pads

Make a small version of the owl template. Cut out the owl body as done for the pin but carve the details in with a pointed tool. Fire and patinate the earrings and polish them. After firing, glue onto flat pad ear posts using two-part epoxy glue.

Pendant

YOU WILL NEED

10g Art Clay silver

Art Clay paper type approx.
¾x ¾in (2 x 2cm)

Art Clay syringe

1 x 8mm Sterling silver jumpring

1 x chain

Make another owl without the pin at the back using the steps in the main project. Add a hole at the top before you fire it. Add a jumpring and thread onto a chain of your choice (see page 26).

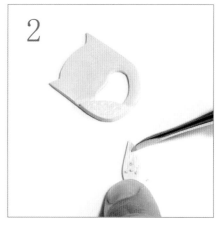

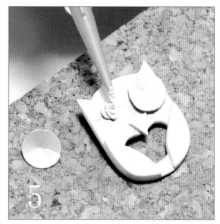

To make a reusable template, cover the front and back of your drawing with clear sticky tape before you cut it out. The tape prevents your template from getting wet and adds stability.

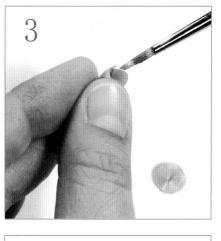

Pin

1 Draw your owl and make paper templates for the body and the wings (height 1in/2.5cm), width ¾in/2cm). Roll the clay ¹⁄₁₆in (1.5mm) thick (see page 20) and cut out the body, the wings, and a beak for the owl with a needle tool. Make a disk ⅛in (2mm) thick with a diameter of ⅜in (9mm) for the pin back. Let all the pieces dry and refine them using your preferred tools (files, sanding pads, baby wipes).

2 The parts should be as smooth as possible. Use a carving tool to carve short grooves into the wings to represent feathers. Add a generous drop of water to where you want a wing to be. Press the wing onto the body and wiggle slightly until you feel the parts grab. Adjust the position and let dry. Add the second wing and the beak. Refine and let it dry.

3 Cut two circles of Art Clay paper with a diameter of ⅜in (9mm). Mark the centers and cut halfway through the circles. Form a cone by overlapping the sides of the cut by ¹⁄₃₂–⅛in (1–2mm). Use a tiny bit of paste to stick the sides together. Let it dry. Add a little bit of syringe to the back of the cut and pad it down with a damp brush to stabilize the cones.

4 Join your disk to the back of your owl. Drill a hole for the pin back (see page 21 for help with drilling). The base of the pin should sit comfortably in the hole with the little prong sticking out. Fill the hole with syringe and press the pin back into it. Use a damp brush to cover it with the syringe that oozed out at the sides. Take care not to cover the prong. Let dry.

5 Make a hole in your support for the pin so your owl can lie flat while you attach the cones. Make pencil marks where you want the center of the owl's eyes to be. Place generous blobs of syringe onto your marks and carefully press the cones into the blobs. Adjust them with the silicone tip of a clay shaper. Let dry. Fire the pin for two hours at 1,472°F (800°C) (see page 23).

6 Brush your owl with a brass brush. You can use the brush of your electric rotary tool to reach into the tight spaces. If you have a tumble polisher, tumble it instead. Make a weak solution of liver of sulfur and dip your owl into the solution until you are happy with the color. Stop the process with cold water (see page 25).

7 Use the silicone tip of your rotary tool to polish the wings, the beak, and the inside of the cones. Be careful not to touch the dark parts with your tools. Turn your owl around and remove the oxidation from the pin and the back using radial bristle discs. Use a burnisher or the silicone tip to bring the sides of the owl to a high shine.

8 Put a little bit of pumice powder onto your work surface. Use a silicone clay shaper and cover the tip with a baby wipe. Dip it into the pumice powder and rub across the inside of the cones until the surface becomes matte. Use radial movements from the center toward the edge. Wash the powder away.

9 For the eyes of your owl, form two tiny balls of black polymer clay and bake them according to the manufacturer's instructions. You can experiment with the size of the eyes to give the owl a different look. Glue the balls into the center of the cones with two-part epoxy glue.

When designing pins and brooches with holes, always keep in mind that the fabric of the clothing becomes part of your design.

Love Birds

This pair of brightly colored birds, inspired by European folk art, was designed by Helen Foster-Turner along with a delicate heart to create a romantic necklace and earrings.

FOR THE NECKLACE YOU WILL NEED

15g Art Clay silver

Art Clay silver paste

7 x fine silver embeddable eyelets

Crystals or beads of your choice

1 x 2in (50mm) silver headpin with shaped end

5 x 6mm jumprings

1 x ready-made silver chain

Tracing paper

Thin polystyrene sheet

Ball burnisher or ballpoint pen

Roller

Playing cards

4¾ x 6in (12 x 15cm) piece of flexible plastic

Badger balm or olive oil

Needle tool or craft knife

Needle file

Foam-backed emery paper

Handheld gas torch

Polish

2 x 2g colored resins

4g resin hardener

Fine glitter (optional)

Small paintbrush or cocktail stick

UV light (optional)

Permanent marker

Necklace

1 Trace the template designs onto tracing paper using a soft pencil. Reverse the tracing paper and retrace the bird image to give you the mirrored image on both sides. Cut the polystyrene sheet into sections large enough to comfortably take each of the designs.

2 Place the tracing paper on the polystyrene sheet and gently draw over the image just hard enough to transfer the design. Use a ball burnisher or ballpoint pen to make the image stand out. Deepen it to get a clear outline. Flip the bird image over for the next mold. Trace the heart onto another piece of the sheet.

3 Roll the clay to five cards thick (see page 20). Lift the rolled clay carefully onto one of the molds, so that it covers the imprint. Place four cards on either side of the design and a thick piece of flexible plastic over the top of the clay. Roll, peel away the clay, and place on a flat surface.

4 Use a needle tool or craft knife to carefully cut around each of the birds and the heart. Place in a warm, dry place to dry off the moisture. Once dry, use a pencil to mark out where to put the eyelets on the beak and tail of the birds and on each side and the bottom of the heart.

5 Use the needle file to make a channel. The channels should be large enough to embed the eyelets but not too deep. Insert the eyelets, cover with thick paste, and smooth down and dry. Let them dry completely and then sand using foam-backed emery paper. before using a torch or placing them in a kiln. Torch-fire for five minutes or kiln-fire for 20 minutes at 1,202°F (650°C) minimum (see page 22). Once fired, cool, polish, and clean to a bright shine.

6 Prepare resins in the colors of your choice, following the manufacturer's instructions. Try out your resins on a piece of white laminated paper or a pocket file with white paper in it. If you are mixing colors you can jot down the mix ratios beside the testers and then pick your favorite. Mix in some glitter to add sparkle.

7 Drip in the resin carefully with a small paintbrush or cocktail stick. Tease it around the eye and spiral details. If you are not sure about the colors on silver, try putting on a thin layer first; you can remove it if you don't like it or, once dry, add another layer that will enhance the colors.

8 Put the pieces on a level surface and let them dry or use a UV light to cure them if you have used UV resins. Once they are dry you can make up the necklace. Attach a fancy headpin, and thread on two or three beads in colors to complement the design. Add a jumpring to each bird's tail (see page 26) and link the heart to the two beaks.

9 Take the chain and mark the center with a permanent marker. Line up the chain against the bird and heart links and ensure the pen mark is over the middle of the heart. Cut out the piece of chain between the two tail eyelets and then connect up the rest of the chain to the jumprings on each tail.

Templates
Printed at actual size.

Earrings

YOU WILL NEED

15g Art Clay silver

Art Clay silver paste

4 x fine silver embeddable eyelets

6 x 2in (50mm) silver-colored headpins

6 x 4mm crystals

6 x 2mm silver beads

2 x silver-colored earwires

2 x 2g colored resins

4g resin hardener

Fine glitter (optional)

Make two mirrored hearts by creating a pattern in the same way as for the birds but add eyelets at the top and bottom. Use silver headpins to make the hanging crystal pieces. Add silver beads either side of a crystal to the headpins and make simple loops at the top (see page 27). Open the loops (see page 26) and attach them to the eyelets. Add three to each heart and then attach the top eyelets to the loops in earwires.

Try out different-colored resins and inclusions before you add them to your project. Match the colors to the beads you have.

Natural Gems

This lovely woodland-themed pendant and matching earrings set by Chu-mei Ho is made with silver clay and cubic zirconia.

FOR THE PENDANT YOU WILL NEED

14g Art Clay silver

Art Clay silver paste

6in (15cm) length of US 20-gauge (SWG 21, 0.8mm) fine silver wire

Two-part silicone-molding compound

Fresh leaves or skeleton leaves

3 x 4mm cubic zirconia (CZ)

16in (40cm) length of fine curb chain

2 x 4mm bicone crystals

4 x 6mm jumprings

1 x clasp

2 x embeddable eyelets

Roller

Cocktail stick

Playing cards

Small circle cutter

Tweezers

Badger balm or olive oil

Clay shaper

Paintbrush

Sanding pads

Brass brush

Agate burnisher or tumble polisher

Liver of sulfur

Round-nose pliers and wire cutters

Glanol metal polish and a silver polishing cloth

Earrings

YOU WILL NEED

10g Art Clay silver

Art Clay silver paste

2 x 3mm cubic zirconia (CZ)

4in (10cm) length of fine curb chain

2 x earwires

To make a pair of matching earrings follow the same steps as for the main project but make smaller twigs and use 3mm CZs. At Step 2 place the eyelets at the top edge on either end instead of in the ends, then continue to follow the steps. You can torch-fire the earrings (see page 22) if they are smaller than 1in (2.5cm). When finished, add 2in (5cm) of fine curb chain to each eyelet and then thread both ends of chain on to an earwire (see page 29). Repeat for the other earring.

Use leaves with small, fine details when making leaf molds.

Do not quench a project with embedded CZs straight after firing.

Pendant

3

6

9

Clean the CZs before firing to avoid silver dust fusing onto the surface.

1 Roll about half the clay out into two small coils with your finger, then roll the ends together on one side and join to create a Y-shape. Use your finger or a clay shaper to shape the coils, so it looks like a twig.

2 Take the two embeddable eyelets and push them into the ends of the twig before the clay becomes dry.

3 Apply a thick layer of silver clay paste onto the twig and use a cocktail stick to create a wood grain texture on the surface. Once it's dry, do the same on the back of the twig.

4 Mix the two-part silicone-molding compound following the manufacturer's instructions. Roll the mixed molding compound to a thickness of $\frac{1}{16}$in (2mm) (8 playing cards). Put a leaf on the molding compound and roll with a roller to take an imprint of the leaf texture. Remove the leaf and let the molding compound set (see page 24).

5 Roll a very small amount of clay into the shape of a teardrop with your fingers and press it onto the lightly greased leaf mold to make a tiny leaf. Make more leaves in the same way.

6 Make some CZ components by rolling the clay out to a thickness of $\frac{1}{8}$in (2.5mm/10 playing cards) (see page 20) and press a 4mm CZ into the wet clay. Make sure the table of the CZ is in line with the clay surface and is level. Use a small circle cutter to cut the clay around the CZ and leave enough clay—at least $\frac{1}{32}$in (1mm)—around the edge. Let dry and sand if needed.

7 Arrange the leaves and CZ components, and join them onto the twig with paste. Once they are dry, turn to the back and use the clay shaper to fill the gaps in between the CZ components and the twig with clay. Create wood grain textures on the back of CZ components using thick paste and a cocktail stick (Step 3) so the textures on the back of the twig are consistent.

8 Kiln-fire the twig pendant at 1,652°F (900°C) for two hours or follow the manufacturer's firing instructions for the minimum firing temperature and time (see page 23). After firing, brush with a brass brush and soapy water. Polish the whole pendant with a tumbler polisher or use an agate burnisher to highlight the textures.

9 Mix some liver of sulfur solution (see page 29) and dip the twig pendant into it until you achieve your desired result. Use metal polish and a cloth to enhance the texture. Add chain to the eyelets with jumprings (see page 29). Cut the chains about 3in (75mm) long on either side of the twig. Cut two 3in (75mm) pieces of wire and follow the technique on page 28 to make wrapped loops on the ends of each. The technique shows the loop being made with a bead attached so just start at step 2 and make the first bend about 1in (2.5cm) along the wire. At step 7 on the wrapped loop technique add the chains that are attached to the twig, one on each side. Add a crystal to each wire and make another wrapped loop above the crystal, again at step 7 add the end of the long piece of chain you have spare. Attaching both ends of the chain to the wrapped crystal sections. Find the middle of the chain and cut or open the link at that point. Add a clasp to one end and a jumpring to the other end using the technique on page 29 for attaching loops.

Woodland Chic

A walk through the woods to observe the colors, textures, and forms of emerging seeds and pods inspired this design by Tracey Spurgin.

FOR THE NECKLACE YOU WILL NEED

20g Art Clay silver

Headpins with ball ends (one per felt ball)

8 links of a large link chain

1 x large jumpring (to fit rubber cord)

1 x 3mm black rubber thong

Roller

Patrik Kusek's Woodland Chic texture plate, from Dynasty Stamps

Badger balm or olive oil

1mm spacer bars

1.5mm spacer bars

½in (1cm) and ¾in (2cm) circle cutters

Tissue blade

Marbles

Coarse sanding grit

1mm drill bit or pin vise

Handheld gas torch

Polishing papers

Tumble polisher or radial discs on a rotary drill

Liver of sulfur

Polish and soft cloth

Marino wool roving or tops

Necklace

1. On a prepared work surface, roll out the clay ¹⁄₁₆in (1.5mm) thick (see page 20). Lightly balm the texture plate. Re-roll the clay using 1mm spacers.

2. Using the two circle cutters, select the area to be cut. Here the focus has been to center each cutter onto the radiating lines of the textures before cutting out.

3. Use a tissue blade to carefully lift the cut circles and gently ease each piece over a selection of marbles, which are being used to create a domed shape. To prevent the marbles from rolling while the clay dries, use a little polymer clay to act as a base on the marble. Set aside all the pieces to dry.

4. Once the pieces are fully dried, you will need to sand each of the component parts. Place the pieces dome-side up on a coarse sanding grit. Rotate the domes in a circle or a figure eight movement to level the leading edges.

5. Use a pin vise or small hand drill to drill a ¹⁄₃₂in (1mm) hole through the center of each of the domes (see page 21). Ideally work from the right side, in order to center the drilled holes. Take care not to put too much pressure down onto the dome, or it could collapse. Next fire all the pieces by using a handheld gas torch or in a kiln at 1,472°F (800°C) for 15 minutes (see page 23).

6. Once fired and cooled, you can begin polishing. Do this by hand or by using a rotary drill with radial disc attachments. To oxidize the pieces, mix together liver of sulfur and warm water and immerse the components for one minute (see page 25). Finally use polish and a soft cloth to buff to a good shine.

7. To make the felt balls, work at a sink with a towel laid in front of you. Use your fingers to draw off a small amount of wool from the main roving. Cup it into the palm of your hands, add a very small amount of liquid soap, and lightly clasp the wool in your hands and immerse in hot water to soak the wool. Remove it from the water.

8. Now cup your hands again and very lightly start to roll the wool in the palm of your hands. Continue until the ball has become matted and firm. As the ball becomes more solid, start applying greater pressure with your hands as you continue to roll until the ball is firm and compact. Rinse out the soap and let dry.

9. Take a headpin and place one of the larger bead caps on the end, then add a felt ball and a smaller bead cap. Make a wrapped loop (see page 28), and then add the loop to the last link on the section of chain before closing the loop (see page 26). Graduate the balls using the larger ones at the bottom. Use a large jumpring to attach the finished piece to the necklace.

Ring

YOU WILL NEED

5g Art Clay silver

Marino wool roving or tops

1 x 2in (50mm) silver headpins with ball ends

Approx. 10in (25cm) length of US 18-gauge (SWG 19, 1mm) wire

Approx. 10in (25cm) length of US 26-gauge (SWG 27, 0.4mm) wire

1 x jumpring

For a ring, wrap 18-gauge wire around a ring mandrel a few times and then wrap the ring in 26-gauge wire to cover the ring wire ends. Make a felt ball as in the main project and add to the ring with a jumpring (see page 26) by pushing the jumpring through a couple of the wire wraps. This will hold the ring in place so it doesn't move to the underside of the ring when you wear it.

Earrings

YOU WILL NEED

5g Art Clay silver

Marino wool roving or tops

2 x 2in (50mm) silver headpins with ball ends

2 x earwires

2 x jumprings

Make a couple of matching felt balls using the main project and attach them to earwires with jumprings for some cute earrings.

These bead caps would look great in copper clay too. Make sure you buy the torch-fireable clay if you don't have access to a kiln.

Metallic Marvel

This modern waterfall design of scrumptious copper and tonal beads by Emma Hall was inspired by falling leaves.

FOR THE NECKLACE YOU WILL NEED

50g Art Clay copper

1 x 18in (460mm) length of medium copper curb chain

1 x copper toggle clasp

13 x copper oval jumprings

12 x copper headpins

12 x beads in assorted shades of brown

Badger balm or olive oil

Roller

Two textures (wallpaper, sandpaper)

Playing cards

Nonstick baking sheet (optional)

Diamond-shaped cookie cutters

Needle tool or cocktail stick

Sponge-backed sanding pads

Pin vise and 1mm drill bit

Fiber blanket

Water basin

Safety pickle

Brass brush

Flat- and snipe-nose pliers

Earrings

YOU WILL NEED

5g Art Clay copper

2 x copper earwires

2 x 1in (25mm) lengths of copper chain

2 x 8mm bicone-shape, brown-colored beads

6 x 8mm copper jumprings

2 x 1in (25mm) copper headpins

Make two small and two tiny copper pieces following the instructions for necklace. Attach the earwires to the chains (see page 29). Make two pieces with the bicones on headpins and create a simple loop (see page 27) above the bead. Attach each one to a jumpring and then hang from the first link on the chain by the earwire. Add jumprings to each of the copper clay pieces and add the large ones to the last link on the chains and the tiny clay pieces to the third link up from the end.

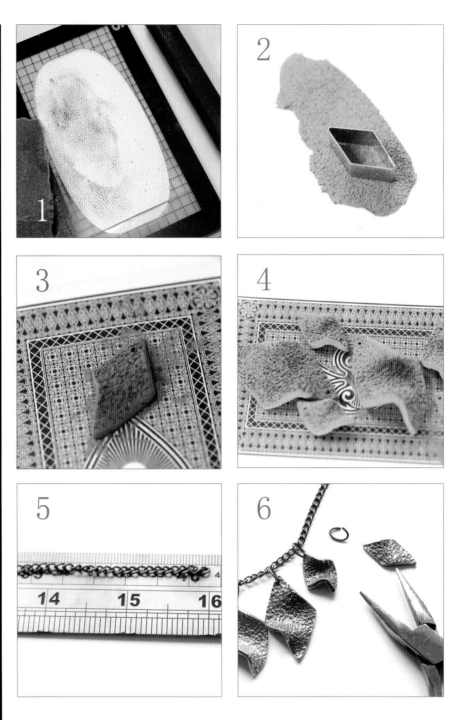

When you open up the clay, knead it through the plastic wrap to make it more pliable before working with it.

Rolling the clay out more thickly helps compensate for the loss through oxidation.

Necklace

1 Apply a little Badger balm, olive oil, or release spray to your textures and roller. You will need two stacks of five cards. Place the copper clay in plastic wrap. Place one texture under your card stacks. Break off a lump of clay and squash it slightly. Place it on top of the texture, and then place the other texture face down upon it and roll firmly to add texture to both sides.

2 Peel the clay from the textures and put it onto a spare playing card or Teflon baking sheet. Lightly oil a diamond-shaped cutter and cut the clay firmly. You can cut a couple of pieces at a time, but be sure to lightly spray with water and cover any you are not working with, using spare plastic wrap. Roll up any spare clay and put it back in the plastic wrap with the rest.

3 Put a hole in the piece about ⅛in (2mm) from the top using a needle tool or cocktail stick. It is a pilot hole so only needs to be rough. Gently grasp each end of the copper shape and twist in opposite directions until the piece curves. If it tears, the clay is not moist enough. Smooth the edges with a damp brush. Dry naturally or use a dehydrator or hot plate.

4 Repeat and make three large center pendants, six medium size and four small diamonds. Smooth the edges and then let them all dry. Gently sand the edges only using sponge-backed sanding pads in three grades, going from rough to smooth. Stroke in the direction of the edge and support the piece with your finger and thumbs. Gently drill through the hole you made in Step 3 to widen and even it up (see page 21).

5 Fire the clay pieces in a kiln using a fiber blanket to support the shapes (see page 23). Follow the manufacturer's recommended firing schedule. You can torch-fire this clay if you wish. While the clay is firing, cut the chain to the length you want and attach the toggle clasp with jumprings to either end of the chain (see page 29).

6 As soon as the kiln is cool enough to open, carefully move the pieces into a bowl of cold water. Handle the metal with tongs as they are still hot. Mix a pickling solution with pickle salts and water; place the copper in the solution and leave for about ten minutes to clean the surface. Wash the pieces with cold water and dish soap after pickling. Brass brush to create a satin finish. Find the middle of the chain and attach a large copper diamond with a jumpring (see page 26); attach the other large diamonds either side. Then spread the smaller ones out each side. Place a bead on each headpin and make simple loops (see page 27). Then attach the beads in between the diamonds directly to the chain.

Wear latex gloves or use a shielding lotion (such as Gloves in a Bottle) to stop your hands blackening. Make sure you get the lotion right underneath your nails.

Lustrous Leaves

Tame your hair on windy days with this bronze, falling-leaf hair ornament by Tracey Spurgin. A matching keyring and bracelet complete the look.

FOR THE BARETTE YOU WILL NEED

100g Hadar's Quick-fire Bronze Clay	Circle cutters
Paper to create template	Carving tools
Badger balm or olive oil	Snake roller
Bowl	Polish
Palette knife	Radial discs on a rotary drill
Water spritz bottle	Goggles and dust mask
Roller	Stiff bristled brush
2mm spacer bars	Gilders paste
Needle tool	

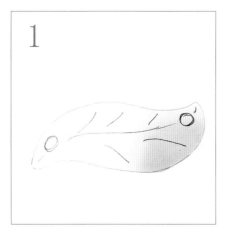

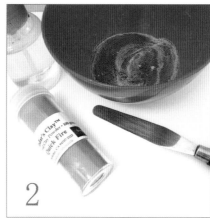

Barrette

1 Start by sketching out the design on paper and cut it out. Apply a generous coverage of Badger balm or olive oil to the paper template. This prevents the paper from sticking to the wet clay.

2 Mix up 100g of Hadar's powder clay with a little water and empty the contents into a bowl. Slowly spritz in water and mix with a palette knife until the clay achieves a crumbly, dough-like consistency. Massage the clay in plastic wrap, cover, and store in an airtight container.

3 Prepare a work surface with a little Badger balm, and roll out the clay to ⅛in (2mm) thick (see page 20). Place the paper template on the clay, then use a needle tool to cut around the outline. Remove the excess and the paper template. Use a circle cutter to cut two holes at opposite ends.

4 To add the gentle arch to the piece, carefully lift and drape the clay over the curve of a bowl. Let the pieces dry.

5 Once the pieces are dry, sketch on a design. Using carving tools, carve out the pattern directly into the dry clay. The bronze remains slightly soft so it carves beautifully. Approach the carving with a steep angle and as you gently move forward with the tool, reduce the angle so the handle is almost parallel with the clay.

6 Take a piece of clay and, using your fingers, start rolling the clay into a torpedo shape. Change to using a snake roller and taper one end of the clay by weighting or favoring one side of the snake roller. When the shape is complete, set aside to dry.

7 The clay needs to be fired in a kiln (see page 23). Hadar Jacobson regularly make updates to the firing times. Check online for information about Hadar's clays.

8 After firing, use a rotary tool and radial discs to clean and polish the bronze. Wear goggles and a dust mask. If you don't have a rotary tool you can use a steel brush instead.

9 To add the final embellishment detail, use gilders paste. To do this, load up a stiff bristled brush with a small amount of gilders paste and apply with a stippling action. Let the gilders paste dry a little, then use a soft cloth to rub off the excess paste. Let dry fully for about 12 hours.

The leftover clay needs to be stored wrapped in cling film in an airtight container with a damp sponge. This helps retain the condition of the clay.

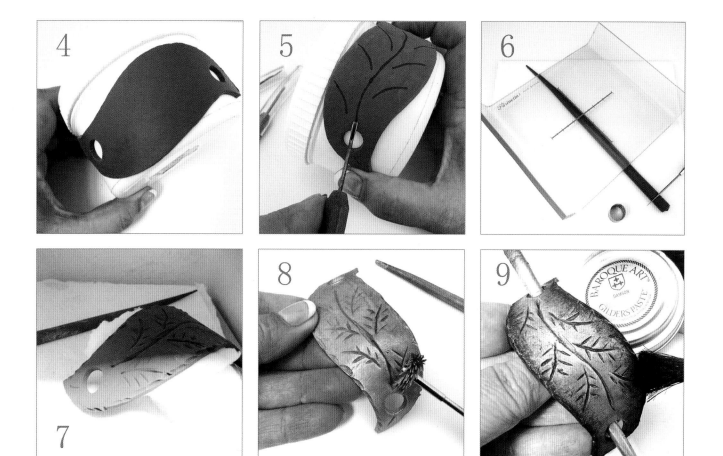

Keyring

YOU WILL NEED

20g Hadar's Quick-fire Bronze Clay

1 x keyring finding

8 x 8mm copper jumprings

Following the same technique to make smaller leaves for a keyring, with a hole only at one end. Attach a jumpring to the keyring (see page 26), then add a jumpring to all three leaves. Take one leaf and attach to the jumpring on the keyring. With the next leaf, add another jumpring to the one on the leaf and attach that to the jumpring on the keyring. For the final leaf, add a set of three jumprings to the one on the leaf and then attach the end ring to the one on the keyring.

Bracelet

YOU WILL NEED

20g Hadar's Quick-fire Bronze Clay

7 x 8mm copper jumprings

1 x copper toggle clasp

Using the same technique to make smaller leaves, make a bracelet by attaching the leaves together with jumprings (see page 26) and finish the piece with a fancy toggle clasp.

Cascading Colors

Be inspired by this pretty mixed-media necklace and earrings set by Lesley Messam.

FOR THE NECKLACE YOU WILL NEED

20g copper clay

20g silver clay

1 x 5mm jumpring made from US 16-gauge (SWG 18, 1.2mm) silver wire

42½in (108cm) length of Sterling silver fine belcher chain

6 x 4mm copper jumprings

15 x 4mm silver jumprings

8 x 8mm bicone crystals

8 x silver ball-ended headpins

Roller

1mm spacer bars

Tile or nonstick work surface

Badger balm or live oil

Leaf texture sheet or fresh leaves

Leaf and flower cookie cutters

Cocktail stick

Playing cards

180, 220, and 280-grit sanding pads

Steel bowl

Brass brush

Silver polish and cloth

Liver of sulfur

Set of pliers and side cutters

Make your own radial texture using
the technique on page 22 with thin
polystyrene sheet.

Necklace

1 Roll out the copper clay out between 1mm spacers, on a tile with badger balm (see page 20). Use a leaf texture sheet or leaves from your backyard. Place the clay in between the textures, pressing firmly. Place the clay back on the tile and cut with a leaf cookie cutter. Using a cocktail stick, make a small hole for hanging. Repeat this step to create ten leaves.

2 Roll out the silver clay between 1mm spacers and two playing cards under each spacer. Remove the playing cards and place a texture sheet on the tile, then the clay. Lay spacers on the texture sheet and then another texture sheet on top. Roll firmly once. Cut out nine small flowers with a cookie cutter and make a small hole in each one. Let dry thoroughly.

3 Once the sections are dried thoroughly, you are ready to sand. Start with 180, 220, and then 280 grits, and make sure you use separate sanding pads for the copper clay. The more effort you put in at this point, the better your finished piece will look.

4 The copper and silver clay cannot be fired together as they turn to metal (a process known as sintering) at different temperatures. Fire the silver clay at 1,436°F (780°C) for a minimum of 15 minutes. Let the kiln cool. Fire the copper at 1,778°F (970°C) for 30 minutes (see page 23).

5 After firing, remove the copper from the kiln and quench (see page 23) in a steel bowl of cold water; this removes the oxidization from the copper.

6 Use a brass brush on the silver. Then go through all the grits once more starting with 180, 220, to 280. Use a silver cloth loaded with silver polish—give a vigorous rub to bring to a high shine. Repeat the sanding with the copper for shiny copper leaves.

7 Make a weak solution of liver of sulfur, then place the silver flowers into the solution until they turn black (see page 25). Remove, wash, and dry. Polish again with a silver cloth loaded with silver polish.

8 Measure and cut a length of small belcher chain to 32in (81cm), then cut another three lengths: 3in (7.5cm), 3½in (9cm), and 4in (10cm). Find the center of the 32in length and attach a 5mm jumpring here (see page 26), add the three shorter chains before closing the jumpring.

9 Attach all the leaves and flowers to 4mm jumprings (see page 26); one ring per piece. Before closing each ring, attach the piece to one of the short chains, then spread the pieces out so they hang nicely. Make wrapped loop pieces with the headpins and bicone crystals using the technique on page 28. Attach each bead to the chains in between the metal pieces using the rest of the jumprings.

Wrap up spare clay quickly to prevent it from drying out.

Earrings

YOU WILL NEED

5g silver clay

5g copper clay

6 x 4mm jumprings

6in (15cm) Sterling silver fine belcher chain (cut in two)

8 x 8mm bicone crystals

8 x silver headpins

2 x earwires

To make the earrings, cut the chain to your desired length then repeat steps 1–9 of the main project. Hang from a pair of earwires using the top link to connect the two (see page 29).

Shine On

This gorgeous silver-clay lentil bead, designed by Rebecca Crabtree, can be decorated with your favorite colored gem.

FOR THE PENDANT YOU WILL NEED

9g PMC3

PMC3 paste and syringe

1 x ceramic bisque lentil bead

2 x 6mm fireable cubic zirconia

1 x thick Sterling silver headpin

1 x Sterling silver bail

1 x Sterling silver snake chain

Cocktail sticks

Badger balm or olive oil

Texture mat

0.5mm spacer bars

Roller

Teflon or other nonstick sheet

Flower cutter

Paintbrush

2mm drill bit

Wire brush

Tumble polisher or burnisher

Wire cutters

Pendant

1 Push cocktail sticks into the hole of the bead, and then using PMC3 paste, paint a layer of silver paste over the entire bead. Let dry, and then add two further coats, leaving to dry thoroughly in between coats. Remove the cocktail sticks and paint inside the holes of the bead with three coats of PMC3 paste.

2 Use Badger balm on the texture mat to ensure that your clay doesn't stick. Place the 0.5mm spacers on top of your texture mat and roll out the PMC3 clay until it is an even thickness (see page 20). Remove from the texture mat, and place down onto a sheet of Teflon. Cut out two flower shapes.

3 Paint a generous amount of water onto the surface of the bead and lay down a flower cutout, making sure all the petals are in contact with the bead. Let the water dry off then repeat on the back with the second flower cutout. Let the whole bead dry.

4 Using the 2mm drill bit, twist the drill into the center of each flower to create a recess. Squeeze some PMC3 syringe into the hole and push the fireable cubic zirconia stone in and adjust to make sure it is straight. Then syringe around the edge of the stone (to create a bezel.) Keep syringing until the height of the bezel has captured the widest part of the stone. Leave to dry.

5 Fire the bead in a kiln at 1,202°F (650°C) for 30 minutes (see page 23). Let the bead cool down inside the kiln. When cold, brush using a wire brush until you achieve a satin sheen all over. Either burnish by hand, or place into a tumble polisher for a couple of hours to achieve a high shine finish.

6 Thread the bead onto the headpin and create a wrapped loop (see page 28). Trim off any excess wire and tuck into the wrapped wire. Open the ring on the Sterling silver bail, thread the wrapped loop through, and close the split ring. Hang from the Sterling silver snake chain.

Earrings

YOU WILL NEED

9g PMC3

PMC3 syringe and paste

2 x 4mm fireable cubic zirconia

2 x 2in (50mm) Sterling silver headpin

2 x Sterling silver long earwires

Use smaller lentil beads to create a matching pair of earrings. Follow the instructions exactly as for the main pendant, but you only need to add the flower to one side of the bead and use a 4mm stone in the center of the flower instead of 6mm. These beads look stunning hung from long V-shape earwires.

To save having to sand the background of the bead, try stippling with some paste and a cocktail stick.

1

2

3

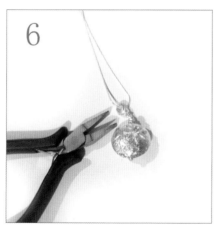

4

5

6

To add extra interest, syringe some vine details onto the bead.

Endless Elegance

Lilies represent elegance, charm, beauty, and grace as shown by these delightful earrings by Julia Rai. Simple to make and very light to wear, they'll look amazing with a matching pendant.

FOR THE EARRINGS YOU WILL NEED

5g Art Clay silver

2 x fine silver embeddable eyelets

2 x Sterling silver earwires

2 x jumprings

Roller

Flat piece of acrylic or old CD case (optional)

Needle tool or craft knife

Playing cards or spacer bars

Small paintbrush

Clay shaper

Sanding pads and polishing papers

Vermiculite or fiber blanket

Tumble polisher or brass/steel brush

Ceramic paint—metallic gold

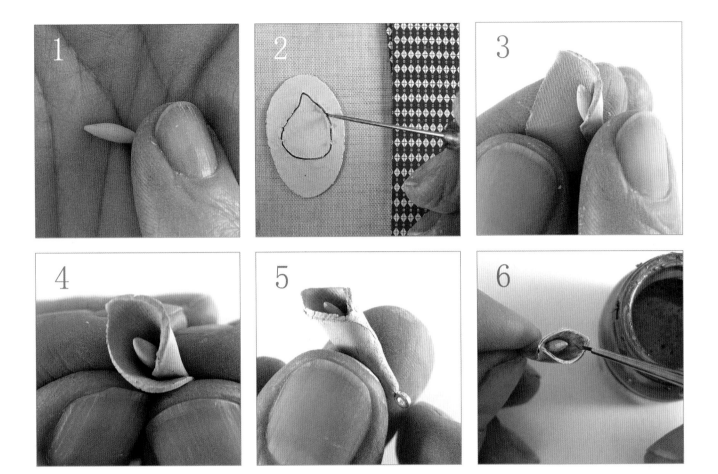

Make these lilies any size you like or even make several in different sizes and combine them to make a bunch.

These earrings are hung upside down but you could solder ear posts onto the back of the lilies and wear them facing upward.

Earrings

1 First make the spadix, the spike-like center of the flowers. Take a small piece of silver clay and roll it into a sausage with a pointed end. You can use a flat piece of acrylic—like a CD case—or just roll it with your finger in the palm of your hand. You need to work quickly so the clay doesn't dry out. Make two and dry them before moving on.

2 The lily flower is formed from a wide teardrop shape. Teardrop cutters are too long and thin so cut this out using a needle tool or craft knife. Cut it freehand—it's a natural form so some individuality is fine—or make yourself a paper pattern to use. Roll out the clay three cards thick, texture if you want to, and cut the shape (see page 20). Do this one at a time.

3 Don't worry if the edges of the cut shape aren't neat; you will clean these up in the dry stage. Take one of the dried spikes and put a little water on the fat end. With the point of the teardrop shape at the top, roll the edge of the teardrop halfway around the spike. The point of the spike should be visible above the rolled edge.

4 Now take the other edge of the teardrop shape and roll it over the outside of the part you've already rolled. Add some water to the part that flaps over and gently press it at the bottom of the flower so it sticks. Smooth the join with a clay shaper. Calla lilies have an open fold over so gently ease the edges of the flower outward around the center spadix.

5 While the clay is moist, push the "key" part of the fine silver eyelet into the base of the flower. Leave to dry and make the other earring. After drying, use sanding pads and polishing papers to refine the edges and surfaces of the flowers. A damp paintbrush will remove small surface imperfections. Fire the clay using a handheld gas torch or a kiln, on a bed of vermiculite or fiber blanket (see page 22).

6 Polish using a brass brush, polishing papers, or a tumble polisher. Burnish the edges of the flowers to add shine. Color the inside of the flower using gold ceramic paint. Apply several coats to give good coverage, letting the paint dry completely between coats. Let dry for at least four hours and bake according to the manufacturer's instructions. Add a jumpring and earwire to each earring (see pages 26 and 29).

If you use a texture on the outside of the earrings, keep it natural. Try using thick paste and stipple it using a finger or a stiff stencil brush for a subtle texture.

Pendant

YOU WILL NEED

5g Art Clay silver

1 x embeddable fine silver eyelet

1 x fine snake chain

The lily shape is perfect for a pendant to match the earrings, hung upside down, and just using a larger eyelet for one lily. Thread the eyelet onto a fine snake chain.

Petal Power

This feminine set of earrings, pendant, and ring by Tracey Spurgin features the natural beauty of a delicate rose.

FOR THE PENDANT YOU WILL NEED

15g PMC Sterling silver clay

Art Clay overlay paste

Badger balm or olive oil

Roller

Playing cards

Needle tool

Files

Sanding grits

Snake roller (flat piece of acrylic or old CD case)

Small pot

Paintbrush

Activated coconut carbon

Container for the carbon

Wire brush

Brass brush

Polishing papers

Tumble polisher or radial disc

Burnisher

Polish and cloth

Round-nose pliers

Liver of sulfur (optional)

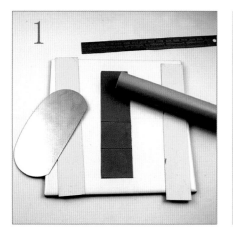
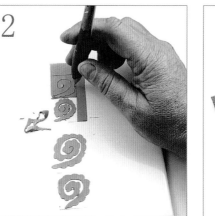

Pendant

1 Prepare your work surface with a little Badger balm. Roll out the clay to one card thick, while making sure the piece has no flaws or cracks and is a consistent thin layer (see page 20).

2 Divide the piece up into sections of two small squares (approx. ¾in/2cm) for the earrings, and two larger squares (approx. 1¼in/3cm) for the ring and pendant rose. Using a needle tool, cut a freehand spiral into the clay as shown, then scallop the outer edge of the spiral following the curve into the center. Remove and store the excess clay and set the spirals aside to dry.

3 Once dry, the pieces are very thin and fragile so minimal handling is needed. Leave the pieces flat and supported on a surface and very lightly sand or file any rough edges away.

4 To make the frame for the pendant, firstly make sure your work surface is clean and free of any balm or oil, as friction is required to roll the clay. Roll out a small amount of clay using a snake roller (this snake was approximately 8in (20cm) long), lightly spray the snake with water, and cover with plastic wrap. Leave to rest for about 1 minute.

5 Remove the plastic wrap from the snake and with a wet brush carefully pick up the snake and coil around a small pot; this will help support the shape while it dries.

6 Once the frame is dry, a little light sanding may be required to refine the edge. To create the rough twig texture, simply apply a little water with a brush to the surface, then use the needle tool to scratch into the surface. Work at this in small sections at a time. Do not over-water the piece. Set aside to dry once more.

7 Fire the frames and rose bases in a kiln (see page 23) (working with Sterling means this will need a kiln to fire). Sit the sections onto a bed of coconut carbon and program the kiln to fire at 1,000°F (538°C) for 30 minutes—leave to go cold before opening the kiln! Do not lift or disturb the pieces but add another layer of carbon (about ¼—½in/5–10mm thick) on top of the pieces and fire at 1,508°F (820°C) for a further 30 minutes, again leaving the kiln to go cold before opening the door to remove the pieces. After removing the pieces from the carbon, lightly wire brush all parts.

8 To create the rose, start at the outer narrow end of the spiral and roll the piece inward toward the center. Make a little Sterling paste or use Art Clay overlay paste to secure the rose to itself. Set aside to dry.

9 There are two options to join the rose and frame together: with either basic silversmithing skills the two can be soldered together, or you could use overlay paste to join them. Once joined, leave to dry. Once dried, return the complete pieces to the kiln for another firing at 1,508°F (820°C) for a further 15 minutes. Bury the piece in carbon once again and let cool before removing. To complete, rub the edges of the rose with the burnisher. To curl the edges of the rose petals, use the pliers to add a little more shape.

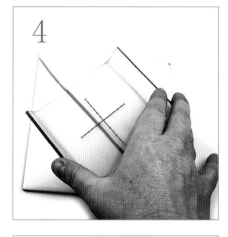

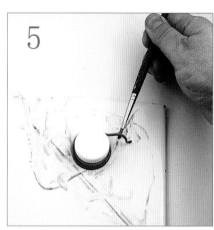

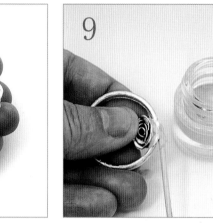

Ring

YOU WILL NEED

15g PMC Sterling silver clay

Pot of overlay paste

The ring band has been made using the same technique as the main project, but with the rose positioned onto the top of the ring band.

Earrings

YOU WILL NEED

15g PMC Sterling silver clay

Pot of overlay paste

4 x 5mm jumprings

2 x Sterling silver earwires

Make smaller versions of the pendant and attach them to earwires with jumprings. Instead of using three jumprings, just use one jumpring and attach it to the hoop, add another jumpring above it and attach that one to the earwire (see pages 26 and 29).

Daisy Delight

Relive lazy childhood days and make this delicate daisy-chain bracelet, designed by Julia Rai. Why not make the matching earrings and hairgrip too?

FOR THE BRACELET YOU WILL NEED

15g PMC Sterling silver metal clay

4 x 6mm jumprings

Approx. 7in (18cm) length of large oval link chain

1 x toggle clasp

Roller

Playing cards or spacer bars

Badger balm or olive oil

Shallow texture mat

Daisy plunger cutters in two sizes

5ml or 10ml measuring spoons

Round brass tube in several sizes

Tweezers

Pin tool or craft knife

600-grit wet and dry sandpaper

Acrylic snake roller or an old CD case

Teflon or other nonstick sheet

Paintbrushes

Activated coconut carbon

Stainless steel container, such as a bean can

Tumble polisher

Soft, clean brass brush

Enamel paint in copper

Ceramic tile

When working with different clays, make sure that you keep tools separate or clean them so you don't contaminate one metal with another.

Bracelet

1 Roll out the PMC Sterling two cards thick onto an oiled shallow texture giving the back of each daisy a subtle pattern (see page 20). Oil the large and small daisy plunger cutters and cut out one large daisy and two small daisies. Oil the inside of 5ml or 10ml measuring spoons and gently put each daisy into its own spoon. This gives each daisy a slightly concave form. Leave to dry naturally.

2 Choose a round brass tube about the same size as the space in the center of each daisy. This will require two different tubes, one each for the large and small daisies. Roll out PMC Sterling two or three cards thick and cut out the circles. Texture each circle using something pointed such as a pin tool so you have a rough surface. While the circle is wet, attach it to the daisy with paste.

3 Once the daisies are dry, carefully remove them from the spoons. They are very fragile so handle them gently. Check the center circles are attached securely all round and add extra paste if necessary, then dry. Use a small piece of wet and dry sandpaper to refine the edges, going all the way down the sides of each petal. The sandpaper allows you to get right into the gaps easily.

4 Using an acrylic snake roller or an old CD case, roll out a very thin snake of PMC Sterling; this one is around ⅛in (3mm) thick and 2½–2¾in (6–7cm) long. Working quickly on a piece of Teflon, use a damp paintbrush to curl the ends around, forming loops that attach to the snake. Use water to join the ends to the snake. This will form the main element of the daisy chain. Let dry.

5 Carefully refine the surface of the dry snake using sandpaper. Make some thick paste in a small pot using PMC Sterling and water. On a sheet of Teflon, turn the largest daisy over so the back is exposed. Using a wet paintbrush, slightly dampen the surface across the middle of the daisy back. Use the paste to securely stick the snake element to the back of the daisy, and then let dry.

6 Make a snake of PMC Sterling that is slightly thinner than the main snake element. While the snake is still moist and pliable, use a damp paintbrush to form a loop at one end and then drape the tail over a brass tube so that it has a "hump" in it. Make the other snake in the same way and let them both to dry over the brass tube.

7 Refine the small snakes with sandpaper. Turn over the large daisy element with the snake attached so the back is facing up. Put the two small daisies under the loops at the end of the big snake elements. Dampen the area directly under the loop on the back of the small daisies and attach the small snakes using paste. Make sure they don't touch the larger loops, and then let dry.

8 PMC Sterling requires two firing phases. Phase one needs air to burn the binder away. Put ½in (1cm) activated coconut carbon in a stainless steel container, then place the piece on top and kiln-fire (see page 23), following the product guidelines (use full ramp to 1,000°F (538°C), hold for 40 minutes). Cool slowly with the kiln door closed. Cover with ½in (12mm) of carbon, put a lid on and fire again (full ramp to 1,499°F (815°C), hold for 45 minutes).

9 Polish using a tumble polisher. Dispense a small amount of enamel paint onto a ceramic tile and with a fine paintbrush, paint the center of the daisies. Paint dries quickly so only dispense a small amount at a time. Let it dry completely. Attach the chain to the loops using jumprings (see page 26) and add a clasp.

Earrings

5g PMC Sterling silver metal clay

2 x fine silver embeddable eyelets

2 x silver earwires

Make matching earrings using the daisy design and embedding fine silver eyelets at the point of one petal. After firing, add earwires.

Hairgrip

15g PMC Sterling silver metal clay

Hairgrip

Make a hair ornament using a small daisy with a snake loop on the back. Make the flower the same way as the main project but don't add an eyelet. To make the snake loop, roll a very thin snake of clay and cut a short section, then dry it over a cocktail stick to make a loop. As soon as it is dry, sand the edges flat and attach to the back of the daisy with a tiny amount of paste. Hold in place for a moment, then let dry again before firing. After firing, attach a hairgrip through the loop.

Sweet Harmony

Music appeals to all generations and cultures. These silver pieces of jewelry by Tracey Spurgin capture the score of a piece of music.

FOR THE PENDANT YOU WILL NEED

10g Art Clay silver

Art Clay paste or syringe

2mm diameter rubber thong necklace in your chosen length

Badger balm or olive oil

Roller

1mm spacer bars and playing cards

Graph paper

Tissue blade

Acrylic rod (optional)

800-grit sanding paper

Small wooden dowel

Needle files

Rubber-tipped tool

Brass brush

Tumble polisher

Music score

Masking tape

UV crystal resin

UV light

Glitter (optional)

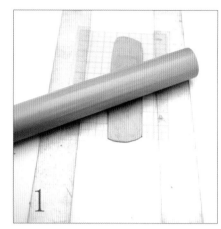
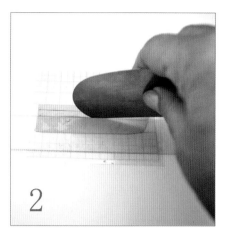
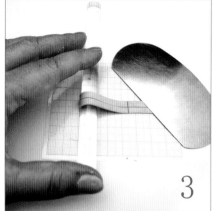

Pendant

1 Lightly oil or use Badger balm on your work surface. Using 1mm spacer bars, roll out the clay to a long thin strip (see page 20).

2 Reference the graph lines on a piece of graph paper to cut two parallel strips of clay. Use a ruler or the space bars to check your cut lines are perfectly straight. Trim off the clay at one end to a 90-degree angle.

3 Using the tissue blade, carefully lift the cut ends and let them drape over an acrylic rod; this could be substituted with a pencil, or the roller. Ensure the two cut ends "hug" the rod and sit on the base card. Level out once again where the clay lands and make a cut at 90 degrees. Set the piece to dry.

4 Once fully dried, separate the two coiled strips. Flip one over so they form a heart shape. Use a file to refine the clay where the two points of contact meet. Use a little paste, or syringe, to adhere the two points together and set aside to dry.

5 Once the piece has dried, lay it flat on a table and very gently begin to sand and level the rim on both sides of the piece, using the sanding paper.

6 To create the loop, roll a coil of clay ¹⁄₃₂in (1mm) thick, apply a little water to let the piece hydrate, then coil a small wooden dowel around the clay. While the clay is still soft, cut through the layers, remove the excess, and nudge the clay so the two coils meet at the cut edges. Set to dry.

7 Once the coil is fully dried, refine with gentle sanding (using needle files), and join the coil bail to the heart using a little paste or syringe. Smooth excess paste off with a rubber-tipped tool. Once again the piece will need to dry thoroughly and may need refining with files. Next, fire following the manufacturer's instructions (see page 22). Polish the fired piece with a brass brush or use a tumbler for a high shine.

8 Lay the heart on the music score and draw around the inside of the heart with a pencil and cut out the paper shape.

9 Take a piece of masking tape and place sticky side up on the back of the silver heart, making sure that the tape covers the whole heart. Place the paper shape music side up inside the heart and press down to make it stick to the tape. Apply a little resin on top of the paper and cure under a UV light. Add glitter if you wish to and then more resin to the top of the silver heart. Cure again and string the heart on a rubber thong necklace.

Earrings

YOU WILL NEED

5g Art Clay silver

2 x 6mm jumprings

2 x silver earwires

A large treble clef mold was made with a button to make these earrings (see page 24). When the mold is ready, take a small amount of clay and press into the mold. Make sure it's level with the top of the mold but don't come over the top too much as you'll just have to sand it all off again. So take your time and try to accurately fill the mold. When the clay is dry, gently press the back of the mold to push the pieces out. Sand and refine them if they need it and then fire. Polish when fired with a brass brush. Take a jumpring and attach the top of the treble clef to an earwire (see page 26); repeat for the other earwire.

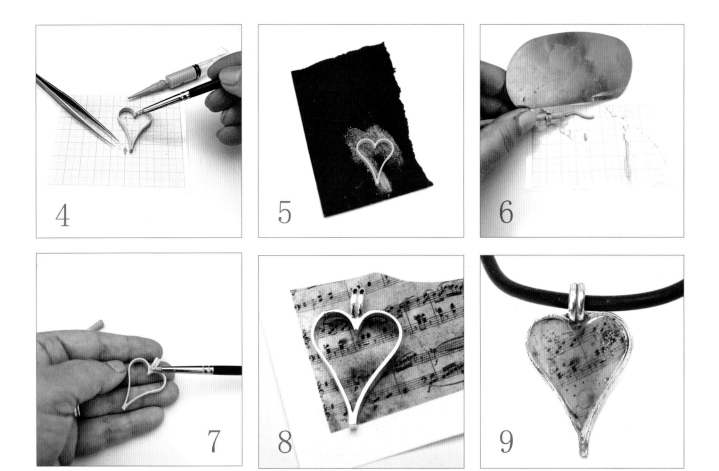

Cufflinks

YOU WILL NEED

15g Art Clay silver

Art Clay paste

Set of embeddable cufflinks

Make a pair of cufflinks with the focal element of the treble clef. Using a tiny treble clef motif button, make a mold (see page 24). When the mold is ready, take a small amount of clay and press into the mold. Make sure it's level with the top of the mold but don't come over the top too much as you'll just have to sand it all off again. So take your time and try to accurately fill the mold, then let dry completely. Roll out a sheet of clay to $\frac{1}{16}$in (1.5mm) thick or 4 playing cards. Texture the front and cut out two squares using a $\frac{3}{4}$in (2cm) square cutter. Lay the squares with the texture side down and push the fireable base mount of the cufflinks into the wet clay. Make sure the texture hasn't been marked and dry the squares. When all the clay is dry, gently press the back of the mold to push the pieces out. Sand and refine all pieces if they need it. Attach the treble clefs to the centers of the squares with a tiny amount of paste. Let dry, then fire and polish. Finish by attaching the bottom of the cufflink pieces into the base mount and lock the cufflink into place.

Leaving the resin for about 15–30 minutes before you cure it will settle the resin. Check for any bubbles before you cure each time.

Resources

UK

Beads Direct Ltd
10 Duke Street
Loughborough
Leicestershire
LE11 1ED
Tel: +44 (0)1509 218028
www.beadsdirect.co.uk

The Bead Shop
44 Higher Ardwick
Manchester
M12 6DA
Tel: +44 (0)161 274 4040
www.the-beadshop.co.uk

Palmer Metals Ltd
401 Broad Lane
Coventry
CV5 7AY
Tel: +44 (0)845 644 9343
www.palmermetals.co.uk

Cooksongold
59-83 Vittoria Street,
Birmingham, B1 3NZ
Tel: +44 (0)845 100 1122
Tel: +44 (0)121 200 2120
www.cooksongold.com

Metal Clay Ltd
27 West Street
Corfe Castle
BH20 5HA
Tel: +44 (0)1929 481541
www.metalclay.co.uk

Bluebell Design Studio
3 Thistle Court
Crossgates
KY4 8AF
Tel: +44 (0)7782 324258
www.bluebelldesignstudio.
co.uk

PMC Studio
87 New Road
Weston Turville
Buckinghamshire
HP22 5QT
Tel: +44 (0)1494 774428
www.thepmcstudio.com

Kernowcraft Rocks & Gems Ltd
Penwartha Road
Bolingey
Perranporth
Cornwall
TR6 0DH
Tel: +44 (0)1872 573888
www.kernowcraft.com

Craftworx
Calf House Studio
Cold Harbour Farm
Bishop Burton
East Yorkshire
HU17 8JF
TR6 0DH
Tel: +44 (0)7961 883115
www.craftworx.co.uk

US

Fire Mountain Gems and Beads
1 Fire Mountain Way
Grants Pass
OR 97526-2373
Tel: toll free 1-800-355-2137
Tel: from UK 1-541-956-7890
www.firemountaingems.com

Hadar Jacobson
Hadar's clays
www.artinsilver.com

Rio Grande
7500 Bluewater Road
NW Albuquerque
NM 87121
www.riogrande.com
Tel: toll free 1-800-545-6566
Tel: from UK 1-505-839-3011

Cool Tools
945 N Parkway Street
Jefferson, WI 53549
Tel: toll free 1-888-478-5060
Tel: from UK 1-323-386-2323
www.cooltools.us

Artclayworld
Art Clay World USA, Inc.
4535 Southwest Highway
Oak Lawn
IL 60453
Tel: toll free 1-866-381-0100
Tel: from UK 1-708-857-8800
www.artclayworld.com

Index

To place an order, or to request a catalog, contact:

GMC Publications Ltd

Castle Place, 166 High Street, Lewes, East Sussex, BN7 1XU

United Kingdom

Tel: +44 (0)1273 488005

Website: www.gmcbooks.com